DELETE

EYEWITNESS
TITANIC

T.S.S.TITANIC

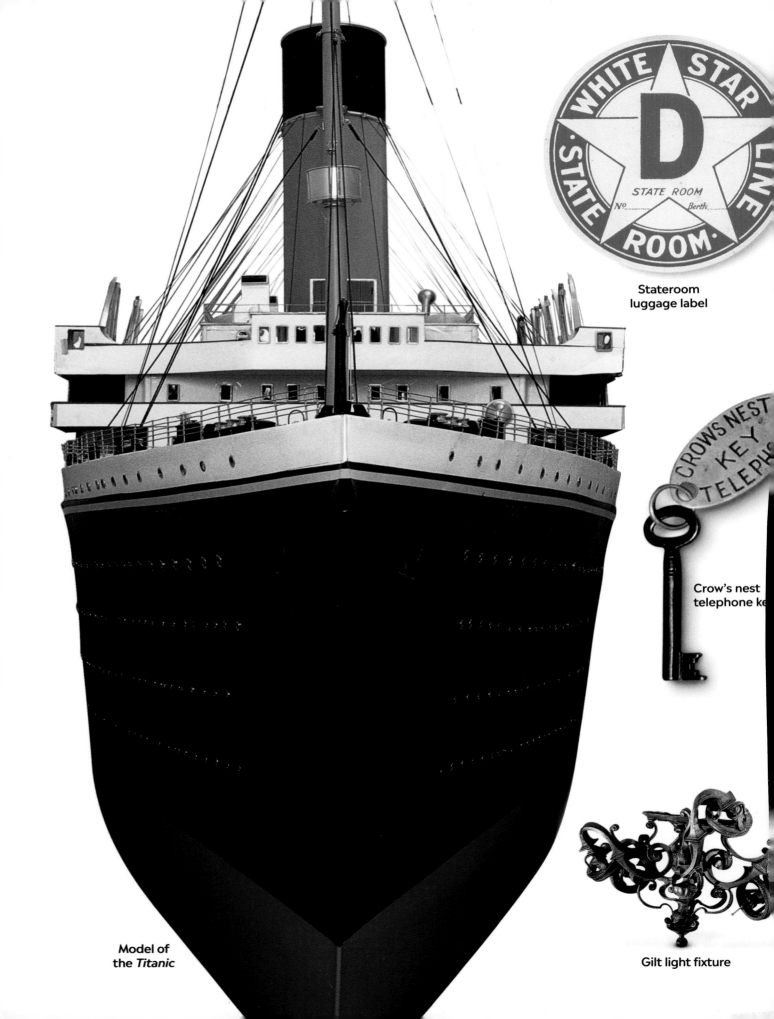

Stateroom
luggage label

Crow's nest
telephone ke

Model of
the *Titanic*

Gilt light fixture

E Y E W I T N E S S

TITANIC

WRITTEN BY
SIMON ADAMS

First-class bath taps

Bell from crow's nest

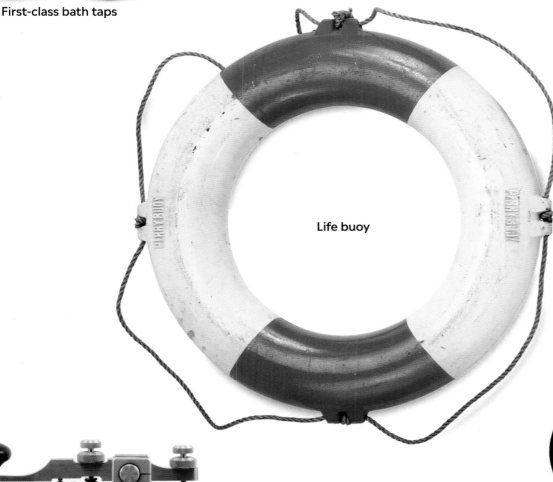
Life buoy

Morse code transmitter

Passageway lamp

FX:8-22

Compass head

Porthole

Captain Smith

DK Penguin Random House

REVISED EDITION

DK LONDON
Senior Editor Carron Brown
Senior Art Editor Lynne Moulding
US Editor Megan Douglass
US Executive Editor Lori Cates Hand
Managing Editor Francesca Baines
Managing Art Editor Philip Letsu
Production Editor Kavita Varma
Senior Jackets Designer Surabhi Wadhwa-Gandhi
Production Controller Samantha Cross
Jacket Design Development Manager Sophia MTT
Publisher Andrew Macintyre
Associate Publishing Director Liz Wheeler
Art Director Karen Self
Publishing Director Jonathan Metcalf

DK DELHI
Senior Editor Shatarupa Chaudhuri
Senior Art Editor Vikas Chauhan
Editor Sai Prasanna
Art Editors Bhavnoor Kaur,
Noopur Dalal, Sifat Fatima
Project Picture Researcher Aditya Katyal
Managing Editor Kingshuk Ghoshal
Managing Art Editor Govind Mittal
DTP Designers Pawan Kumar,
Mohammad Rizwan, Rakesh Kumar
Jacket Designer Juhi Sheth

FIRST EDITION
Project Editor Melanie Halton
Art Editor Mark Regardsoe **Designer** Polly Appleton
Senior Managing Editor Linda Martin
Senior Managing Art Editor Julia Harris
Production Kate Oliver
Picture Researcher Claire Taylor
DTP Designer Andrew O'Brien

This Eyewitness ® Book has been conceived by
Dorling Kindersley Limited and Editions Gallimard

This American Edition, 2021
First American Edition, 1999
Published in the United States by DK Publishing
1450 Broadway, Suite 801, New York, NY 10018

Copyright © 1999, 2004, 2009, 2014, 2021
Dorling Kindersley Limited
DK, a Division of Penguin Random House LLC
21 22 23 24 25 10 9 8 7 6 5 4 3 2
003–314466–Dec/2021

A catalog record for this book is available from the Library of Congress.
ISBN 978-0-7440-3965-8 (Paperback)
ISBN 978-0-7440-2897-3 (ALB)

DK books are available at special discounts when purchased in bulk
for sales promotions, premiums, fund-raising, or educational use.
For details, contact: DK Publishing Special Markets,
1450 Broadway, Suite 801, New York, NY 10018
SpecialSales@dk.com

Printed and bound in China

For the curious
www.dk.com

Logometer

Memorial badge

Compass stand

Contents

White Star Line
playing cards

Ocean travel

In the days of sail, ships took weeks, if not months, to travel between continents. The development of large, fast steamships during the mid-1800s allowed people to cross the ocean more quickly and cheaply than ever before. Shipyards started to build vast, luxurious passenger ships called liners to attract high-paying passengers. It was into this competitive world that the *Titanic* was launched.

Statue of Liberty overlooks New York Harbor

Ornate marble pillars

Luxury liners

No expense was spared in decorating the Atlantic liners. For first-class passengers, the public rooms and cabins were often furnished in the style of great country houses with hardwoods, marble, and gilt. For second-class passengers, the rooms were more than adequately furnished, while many third-class passengers were introduced to good standards of hygiene and table linen for the first time in their lives.

Liberty beckons

Many of the steerage (third-class) passengers on board the North Atlantic liners were escaping poverty and oppression in Europe. Between 1900 and 1914, more than 12 million people sailed from Europe to start a new life in the Americas.

> **"Everything has been done ... to make the first-class accommodation more than equal to that provided in the finest hotels on shore."**
> —**Extract from *The Shipbuilder***

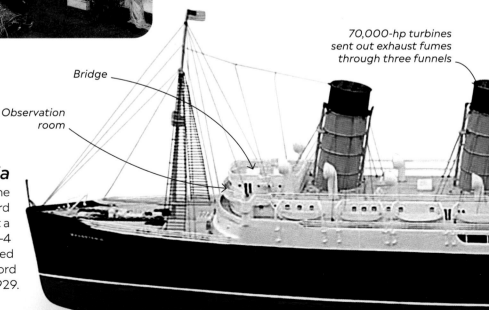

70,000-hp turbines sent out exhaust fumes through three funnels

Bridge

Observation room

Mauretania

With its four giant steam turbines, the *Mauretania* was the pride of the Cunard Line (see p.7). In 1907, the *Mauretania* set a new record for crossing the Atlantic—4 days and 19 hours, at an average speed of 27.4 knots (31½ mph). The record went unchallenged until 1929.

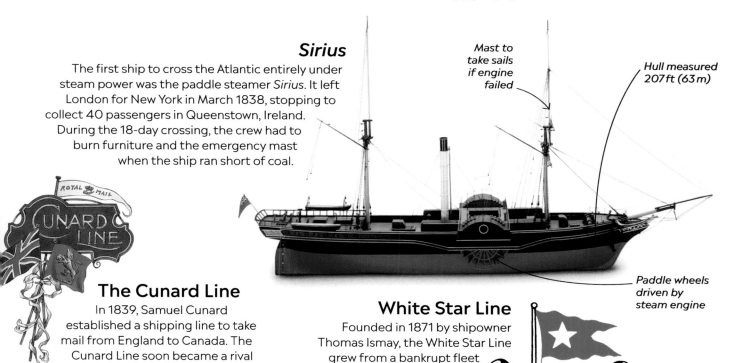

Sirius

The first ship to cross the Atlantic entirely under steam power was the paddle steamer *Sirius*. It left London for New York in March 1838, stopping to collect 40 passengers in Queenstown, Ireland. During the 18-day crossing, the crew had to burn furniture and the emergency mast when the ship ran short of coal.

Mast to take sails if engine failed

Hull measured 207 ft (63 m)

Paddle wheels driven by steam engine

The Cunard Line

In 1839, Samuel Cunard established a shipping line to take mail from England to Canada. The Cunard Line soon became a rival for the White Star Line.

White Star Line

Founded in 1871 by shipowner Thomas Ismay, the White Star Line grew from a bankrupt fleet of clipper ships operating between Britain and Australia.

Red Star Line

The Red Star Line ran steamships from Belgium to America. The line was part of the International Mercantile Marine Company, which also owned the White Star Line, soon to build the *Titanic*.

👁 EYEWITNESS

Shipping tycoon
US industrialist John Pierpont Morgan was one of the richest men of his time. In 1902, he bought a number of European shipping lines and created the International Mercantile Marine Company that came to dominate shipping across the North Atlantic. The White Star Line, which owned the *Titanic*, was part of this company.

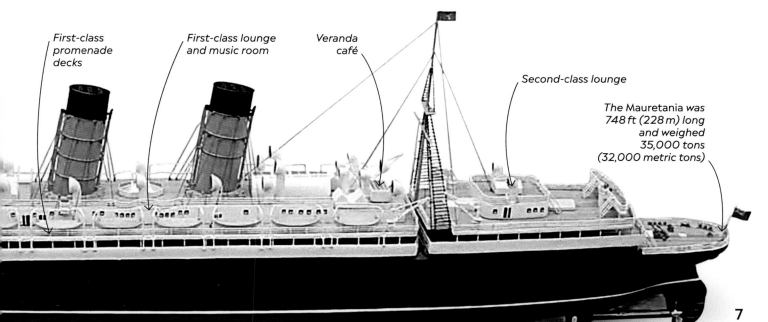

First-class promenade decks

First-class lounge and music room

Veranda café

Second-class lounge

The Mauretania was 748 ft (228 m) long and weighed 35,000 tons (32,000 metric tons)

Building the *Titanic*

Ever since its foundation in 1871, the White Star Line had ordered its new ships from the Harland and Wolff shipyard in Belfast, Northern Ireland. The construction skills of the yard were outstanding, and the workforce took great pride in their ships. Construction of the *Titanic* began on March 31, 1909. First, the keel plates were positioned. Then, when the framework was in place, the beams, deck plates, and hull plates were installed. By May 1911, less than two years after work began, the *Titanic* was ready to be launched.

Under construction
The *Olympic* (right) and the *Titanic* (left) were so big that special slipways had to be built. A central crane and 16 movable cranes were also installed.

The ship was designed with three funnels, but a fourth was added to make it look impressive

Entrepreneur
Lord William Pirrie (right), chairman of Harland and Wolff, had worked for the company since 1862. In 1907, Lord Pirrie and Bruce Ismay, chairman of the White Star Line, planned to build three magnificent liners. Before the *Titanic* had sailed, Lord Pirrie claimed that such luxury liners were unsinkable.

Giant anchor

The *Titanic's* central anchor was the biggest of the ship's three anchors. It took a team of 20 horses to haul it to the shipyard. The two side anchors were half the weight of the central anchor and were lowered by 107 tons (97.5 metric tons) of cable.

Anchor weighed 17 tons (15.75 metric tons)

Thriving workforce

Harland and Wolff doubled its usual workforce of about 6,000 people to cope with the construction and outfitting of the *Titanic* and its sister ship, the *Olympic*. Most of the workers lived in the maze of streets surrounding the dockyard.

The central propeller shaft awaits the huge, bronze propeller

Driving force

Three huge turbine shafts connected the engines to the propellers at the rear of the ship. The outer propellers had three blades, while the central propeller had four.

"a waste of money ...
she's too big ... she'll bump into summat ...
no ship's unsinkable ..."
—Sir J. Bisset

In dry dock

After its launch on May 31, 1911, the *Titanic* went to the fitting-out basin, where the ship's machinery was installed and the inside of the ship was completed. On February 3, 1912, the *Titanic* went to the dry dock, where the propellers were added and a final coat of paint was applied.

"Unsinkable"?

Despite popular belief, the *Titanic's* designers never claimed the ship was unsinkable or exceptionally fast. Its owners claimed that the ship's system of watertight bulkheads (wall-like partitions) "made the vessel virtually unsinkable." The word "virtually" was soon forgotten, however, as the sheer size and luxury of the *Titanic* led most people to believe that the ship truly was unsinkable.

> **"I cannot imagine any condition which would cause a ship to founder. I cannot conceive of any vital disaster happening to this vessel."**
> **—Captain Smith**

Giant boilers

The ship's engines were powered by 29 boilers containing 159 furnaces. The furnaces used 728 tons (660.46 metric tons) of coal a day, driving the ship at a top speed of about 23 knots (42 kph). Here, the boilers are seen lined up in the boiler shop before being installed in the ship's hull.

Massive A-frame supports engine

Some boilers weighed more than 110 tons (100 metric tons)

Mighty engines

The *Titanic* was driven by two massive steam engines, which stood more than 30 ft (9 m) tall. Steam from these two monsters passed into a 470-ton (426.76–metric ton) turbine engine, then traveled along the turbine shaft, providing the power to drive the central propeller.

33-ft (10-m) gaping hole in Arizona's crumpled bow

Surviving the ice

In 1879, *Arizona*—the largest liner of its day— hit an iceberg head-on off the coast of Newfoundland. The bow shattered, but the ship managed to limp backward to Newfoundland without casualties.

THE BULKHEADS

The *Titanic's* 15 watertight bulkheads divided the ship into 16 compartments. In theory, the ship would still float with two compartments flooded, or even with all four of the smaller bow compartments flooded. However, the bulkheads reached only 10 ft (3 m) above the waterline, which meant that water could still slop over from one compartment to another if the ship was sinking.

The Titanic's *15 bulkheads separated its hull into compartments*

Watertight doors

The *Titanic's* bulkheads contained a series of watertight doors. Only 12 of these doors, at the bottom of the ship, could be closed electrically from the bridge. The other 30 had to be closed by hand. After the collision, a few of these manually operated doors were closed, some were left open, and others were reopened to set up water pumps.

Watertight doors drop into place to seal bulkheads

Ticket to the launch of the Titanic

Launch time

The *Titanic* was launched with little fanfare at 12:14 pm on May 31, 1911. Lubricated with soft soap, tallow (animal fat), and tallow mixed with oil, the ship took 62 seconds to slide into the water. Once afloat, tugs pulled it toward its fitting-out berth, just as they had done with the *Olympic* (above) seven months earlier.

Privileged viewers

Most people viewed the launch of the *Titanic* from the banks of the Lagan River in Belfast, but those who had tickets could watch the events from within the dock.

11

RMS *Titanic*

Titanic postcard, 1912

Almost identical to its sister ship, the RMS *Olympic*, the *Titanic* was truly vast. The ship could carry up to 3,547 passengers and crew. When fully laden, the *Titanic* topped 73,924 tons (67,063 metric tons), making it the heaviest ship afloat at that time. The style and luxury of the internal fittings meant that it was also the finest. Its title of RMS—Royal Mail Ship—was highly suitable for such a regal ship.

Ensign of the White Star Line

Wireless aerial strung between two masts

Backstay to hold up rear mast

Rear mast

Second-class enclosed promenade

Docking bridge for use by crew when ship docking in port

Aft deck for use by third-class passengers

Poop deck for use by third-class passengers

Blue Ensign of the Royal Naval Reserve

Third-class cabins in noisy rear of ship

Cast-steel rudder

Central, ahead-only, four-bladed propeller made of bronze

Three-bladed side propeller of bronze

Double-bottomed hull

How long?

The distance from the ensign mast at the stern to the forestay fitting at the bow measured 882.9 ft (269.1 m), or the length of 22 buses.

Breath of fresh air

Passengers could stretch their legs and enjoy the sea air on the boat decks. Deckchairs were available for those wishing to sit and relax, although the lifeboats restricted the view of the sea.

> "Perhaps the most striking features ... are the four giant funnels ... which tower
> # 175 ft (53 m)
> from the keel plate ..."
> —Extract from the *Southampton Pictorial*

Big ship

The sheer size of the *Titanic* remains impressive to this day, but so, too, does the design. The hull was sleek and sheer, dominated by four huge funnels. The two wooden masts were used only as flagpoles for the ensigns (flags) and as supports for the wireless aerial.

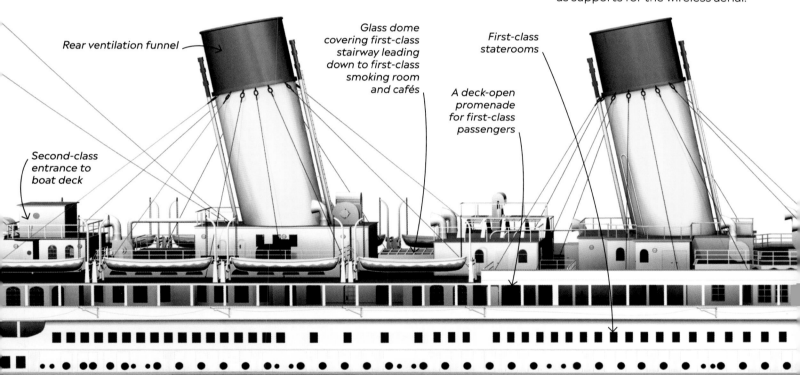

Rear ventilation funnel

Glass dome covering first-class stairway leading down to first-class smoking room and cafés

First-class staterooms

A deck-open promenade for first-class passengers

Second-class entrance to boat deck

On the bridge

Situated at the front of the boat deck, the bridge was the command center of the ship. The captain and his officers surveyed the sea from the bridge and sent orders to the engine room. Although the ship was steered from the wheelhouse, the captain also had a small wheel on the bridge to use in emergencies.

Portholes

Portholes lined the sides of the ship from the first-class suites on C deck down to the third-class berths on the lower deck. The portholes allowed light and fresh air into the cabins and lit up the hull at night.

"Take the **dining saloon**— *Olympic* didn't even have a carpet but the *Titanic*—ah, you sank in it up to your knees."
—Baker Reginald Burgess

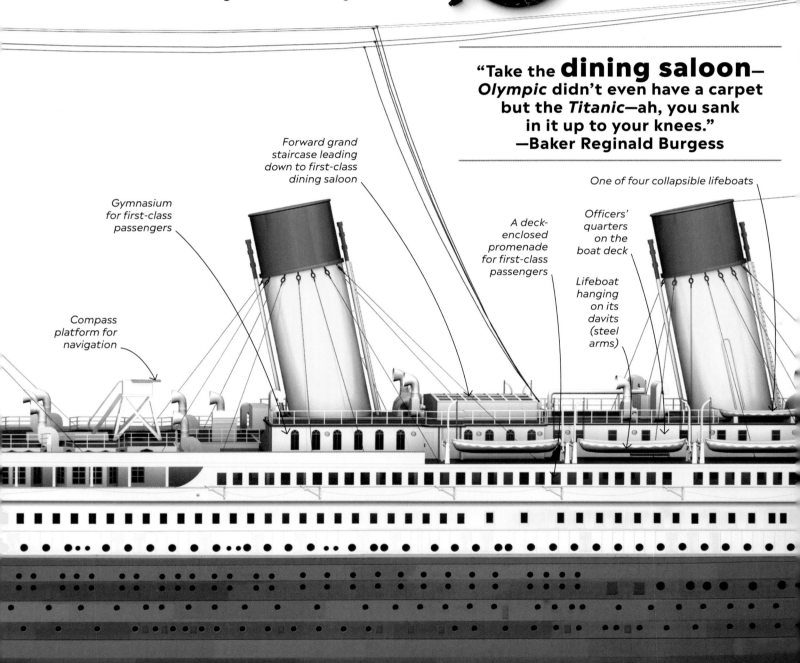

Gymnasium for first-class passengers

Compass platform for navigation

Forward grand staircase leading down to first-class dining saloon

A deck-enclosed promenade for first-class passengers

One of four collapsible lifeboats

Officers' quarters on the boat deck

Lifeboat hanging on its davits (steel arms)

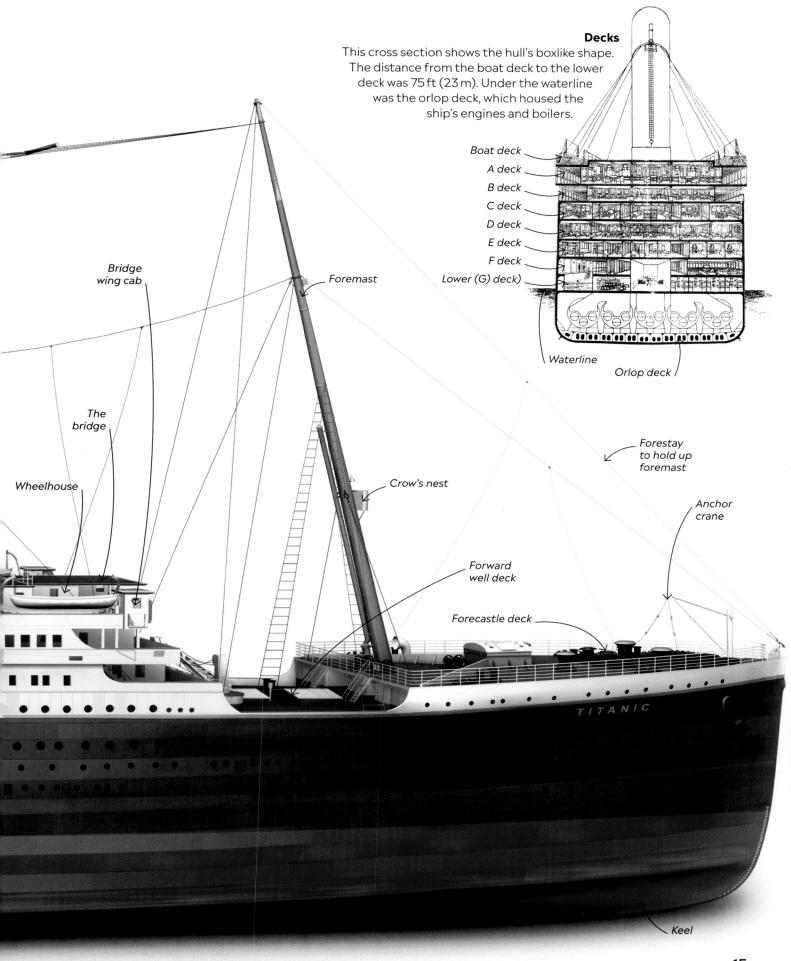

Decks
This cross section shows the hull's boxlike shape. The distance from the boat deck to the lower deck was 75 ft (23 m). Under the waterline was the orlop deck, which housed the ship's engines and boilers.

Boat deck
A deck
B deck
C deck
D deck
E deck
F deck
Lower (G) deck)

Waterline

Orlop deck

Bridge wing cab

Foremast

The bridge

Wheelhouse

Crow's nest

Forestay to hold up foremast

Anchor crane

Forward well deck

Forecastle deck

TITANIC

Keel

Fine fittings

In its fitting-out basin, the *Titanic* was transformed into a floating palace in little more than eight months. No expense was spared in making the *Titanic* the most luxurious liner afloat. All the fittings were bought brand-new or specially made for the ship, and everything was designed to keep the passengers comfortable and entertained during the trip.

Proud to supply

The *Titanic*'s suppliers were proud to associate themselves with the ship. The message in this advertisement was clear: you, too, can share some of the *Titanic*'s luxury, even if you cannot afford to sail on it.

Painter adds highlights to features on a decorative column

Rails of wrought iron and gilt bronze

Ornate columns of polished oak

Gold-plated and crystal light fixtures lit up each landing of the grand staircase

Finishing touches

This photograph shows expert plasterers and decorators at work on the *Titanic*'s sister ship, the *Olympic*. Period detail was lovingly recreated in the first-class rooms and cabins.

Late-17th-century-style cherub lamp support

Grand staircase

The grand staircase led from the first-class dining saloon on D deck up to the first-class promenade deck. The staircase was lit from above by natural light through a glass dome, and illuminated at night by gold-plated crystal lights.

On tap

Every cabin had running water, a luxury few of the third-class passengers would have enjoyed at home. However, there were only two bathtubs for the 710 third-class passengers.

First-class bath taps recovered from the Titanic wreck site

On the veranda

One of the most popular rooms on board was the veranda café. The café was bright and airy, with wicker furniture, a checkered floor, and ivy growing up trellises on the walls.

Reading room

With plenty of space and comfortable chairs, the white-paneled reading room was an ideal place to write a letter or read a book from the selection available in the ship's large library.

Clock surrounded by two figures symbolizing Honor and Glory crowning Time

Gilt light fixture crumpled in wreck

Light fantastic

The gilt light fixtures in the first-class lounge matched the Louis XVI style of the room.

Lift off

Three elevators took first-class passengers from the promenade deck to their cabins. The elevators were magnificently decorated and well disguised behind pillars. An elevator near the stern of the ship was available to second-class passengers.

Captain and crew

Hidden from view was a vast army of workers who kept the ship running. Engineers, chefs, barbers, and many others worked away on the lower decks. On the public decks, stewards, pursers, and waiters took care of the passengers. There were 289 firemen and stokers who shoveled coal into the boilers to keep the engines working at full speed. In total, there were 898 crew members, including the captain and his senior officers, who were responsible for every aspect of life on board.

The power houses

A team of 28 engineers ran the ship's boiler rooms that were hot, noisy, and dirty. If the boilers ran out of coal or stopped working, the ship would grind to a halt.

Chief Purser Herbert McElroy

Second Officer Charles Lightoller

Third Officer Herbert Pitman

Fourth Officer Joseph Boxhall

Fifth Officer Harold Lowe

Sixth Officer James Moody

Chief Officer Henry Wilde

Captain Edward Smith

First Officer William Murdoch

The officers

This photograph shows the captain and his officers on board the *Titanic*. The stripes on the sleeves show an individual's rank—the more stripes, the more senior the officer.

Sam Collins

While on the *Carpathia*, fireman Sam Collins (above) met Frankie Goldsmith, who told him about watching firemen in the *Titanic*'s engine rooms.

Loading mail sacks onto the Titanic

Mail ship

The *Titanic* carried mail for the British Royal Mail. Mail sacks were stored in the hold with the luggage. The five clerks working in the hold were among the first to notice water pouring in through the hull.

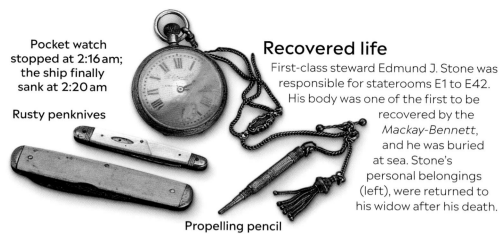

Pocket watch stopped at 2:16am; the ship finally sank at 2:20am

Rusty penknives

Propelling pencil

Recovered life

First-class steward Edmund J. Stone was responsible for staterooms E1 to E42. His body was one of the first to be recovered by the *Mackay-Bennett*, and he was buried at sea. Stone's personal belongings (left), were returned to his widow after his death.

At your service

The first-class restaurant was run by Monsieur Gatti, the owner of an exclusive French restaurant in London. Only one of his team of 55 cooks and waiters survived the tragedy.

"The night before sailing I asked my wife to put my white star in my cap, and while she was doing it **the star fell all to pieces.**"
—Steward Arthur Lewis

Violet Jessop

Annie Robinson

Some of the surviving stewardesses pictured on their arrival in Plymouth, England

The stewardesses

Out of a crew of 898, there were only 18 stewardesses. Attitudes toward women at that time meant that shipping companies employed mostly male staff. But the "women and children first into the lifeboats" rule ensured that 17 of the stewardesses survived the disaster.

Children's toys hang from the ceiling

Souvenir pennants

Reclining chair

Barber shops

Two barber shops (one in first class, the other in second) offered men a daily hot lather and shave. The shops also sold toys, postcards, and other souvenirs.

On record

Fireman William Nutbeam was one of only 35 out of the 167 firemen to survive the voyage. His logbook states "vessel lost" against the *Titanic* entry.

LOOKING FRD.

Collision occurred below the waterline, some 85 ft (26 m) from the stern

Predicting the tragedy

There are many strange stories relating to the *Titanic*. Some are tales of prediction that uncannily described the real-life events of the tragedy. A number of people had recurring dreams of the forthcoming collision, and a dying girl in Scotland related the events of the disaster just hours before they unfolded. Several people had such strong premonitions that they refused to board the *Titanic*. Others were simply very lucky and failed to board on time.

A bad omen

A warning of the forthcoming tragedy occurred on September 20, 1911, when the *Titanic's* sister ship, the *Olympic*, collided with the warship HMS *Hawke*. Both ships were badly damaged, and the *Olympic*, under E. J. Smith, soon to captain the *Titanic*, was found to be at fault.

Vision of death

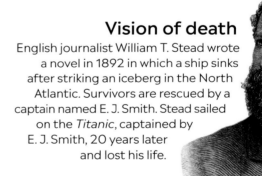

William T. Stead

English journalist William T. Stead wrote a novel in 1892 in which a ship sinks after striking an iceberg in the North Atlantic. Survivors are rescued by a captain named E. J. Smith. Stead sailed on the *Titanic*, captained by E. J. Smith, 20 years later and lost his life.

Collision visions

New York lawyer Isaac Frauenthal had a dream about the disaster before boarding the *Titanic*, and again when he was aboard the ship. Unlike other passengers, he wasted no time boarding a lifeboat when he heard about the collision.

Jessie's dream

On April 14, 1912, a dying Scottish girl called Jessie had a vision of a ship sinking and "someone called Wally ... playing a fiddle." Within hours of her death, the *Titanic* slowly sank as Wally Hartley and the rest of the band continued to play.

Futility

In 1898, Morgan Robertson wrote a novel called *Futility* in which a ship tries to cross the Atlantic in record time, hits an iceberg, and sinks with the loss of almost all of its passengers due to a shortage of lifeboats.

The Belvedere Arms, a pub in Southampton where people were recruited to work on the Titanic

"That ship is going to sink before it reaches America ..."
—Mrs. Blanche Marshall

Missing the boat

Many crew members were recruited in the pubs of Southampton, England. However, 22 recruits failed to board the ship, notably the three Slade brothers, who were prevented from reaching the ship by a long goods train passing through the docks.

The collision depicted in Frank Leslie's Illustrated Newspaper *on April 12, 1856*

Similar fate

In 1856, *John Rutledge* was journeying from Liverpool to New York when it collided with an iceberg on February 19. The passengers boarded lifeboats as the ship sank, but all except one died, either due to the freezing cold or starvation. Thomas W. Nye was rescued by *Germania*.

Lucky escape

Founder of a famous chocolate company, Milton Hershey had booked a first-class stateroom on the *Titanic*. However, he canceled it at the last minute as he had to travel back sooner for work, boarding the SS *Amerika* instead. His narrow escape was reported in the newspaper *The Daily New Era* in Lancaster, PA.

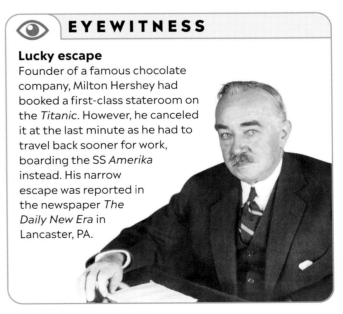

Maiden voyage

South Western Hotel

A number of wealthy passengers spent the night before the voyage in the South Western Hotel, Southampton, overlooking *Titanic*'s dock.

A new ship's first voyage—its maiden journey—is always an important occasion. The *Titanic* arrived in Southampton on April 3, 1912. For the next few days, the docks bustled with activity as the crew arrived and supplies were loaded on board. On the morning of April 10, passengers boarded the ship. At noon, the ship slipped its moorings and the voyage had begun.

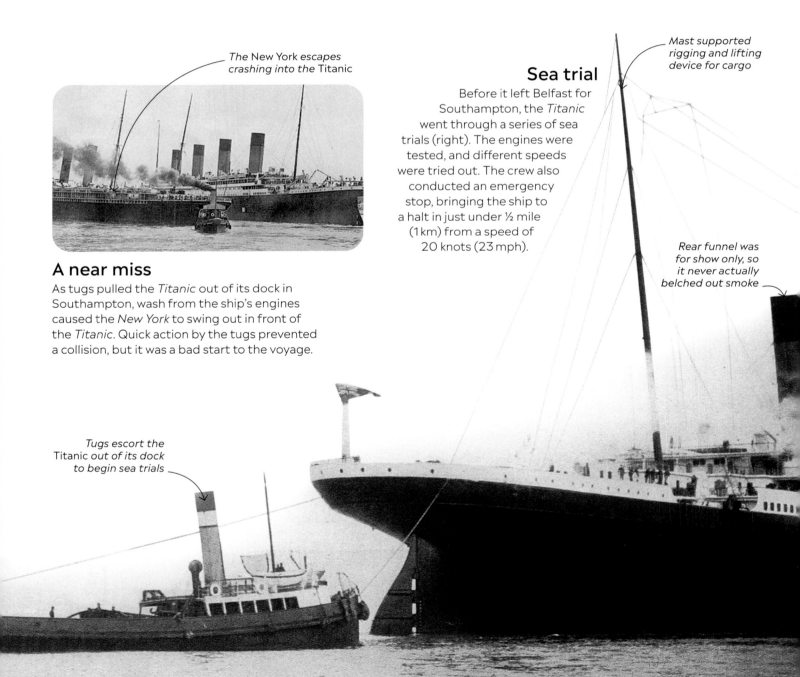

The New York *escapes crashing into the* Titanic

Sea trial

Before it left Belfast for Southampton, the *Titanic* went through a series of sea trials (right). The engines were tested, and different speeds were tried out. The crew also conducted an emergency stop, bringing the ship to a halt in just under ½ mile (1 km) from a speed of 20 knots (23 mph).

Mast supported rigging and lifting device for cargo

Rear funnel was for show only, so it never actually belched out smoke

A near miss

As tugs pulled the *Titanic* out of its dock in Southampton, wash from the ship's engines caused the *New York* to swing out in front of the *Titanic*. Quick action by the tugs prevented a collision, but it was a bad start to the voyage.

Tugs escort the Titanic *out of its dock to begin sea trials*

All aboard
On the morning of the *Titanic*'s departure, huge crowds gathered to wave goodbye to friends and relatives.

White Star Line's Southampton pier on the morning before the Titanic *departs*

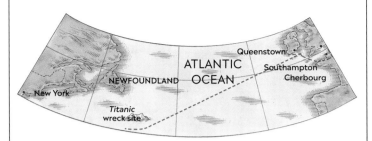

The *Titanic* stopped first at Cherbourg, France, where more passengers got on. It then recrossed the English Channel to Queenstown (now Cobh), Ireland. On April 11, the *Titanic* finally left Europe for New York.

Quality luggage was an essential fashion accessory for wealthy passengers

Strong locks to keep contents secure during voyage

Farewell to Europe
At Queenstown, the *Titanic* picked up seven second-class and 113 steerage (third-class) passengers, many of whom were leaving Ireland to start a new life in America.

> "The ship is so big that I have not yet found my way about.
> # I hope I shan't get lost on board
> before I arrive in New York!"
> —A passenger

First class

With most of the top four decks reserved for their use only, the 329 first-class passengers sailed in lavish comfort, with a vast workforce ready to cater to their every need. When not resting in their cabins, first-class travelers had the use of a squash court; a gymnasium; a swimming pool; a library; and a range of dining rooms, bars, and restaurants.

À la carte

This menu for the last luncheon served on the *Titanic* shows the choice of dishes on offer. The first-class dining room could seat more than 550 people.

The mechanical camel was especially popular

Keep in shape

The gymnasium contained rowing and cycling machines, weights, and other equipment to keep the first-class passengers fit.

Dinner and dance

The seven-course evening meal was the social highlight of the day. Women wore their finest new gowns from Paris; the men wore evening suits. After the meal, the more energetic passengers took to the dance floor. Other men retired to the smoking rooms, and women to the various lounges.

Tables decorated with fresh flowers and baskets of fruit

Starched white linen napkins and tablecloths

Luggage labels

Every item of luggage was carefully labeled. First-class passengers often took large quantities of belongings. Mrs. Charlotte Cardeza, for example, traveled with 14 trunks, 4 suitcases, 3 crates, and a medicine chest.

In state

The first-class staterooms (private cabins) were very spacious, particularly the two promenade suites on B deck. These suites included a sitting room, two bedrooms, two dressing rooms, a bathroom, and a private deck.

French Empire–style chairs and table

> **"My pretty little cabin with its electric heater and pink curtains delighted me ... its beautiful lace quilt, and pink cushions, and photographs ...**
> # it all looked so homely."
> **—Lady Duff Gordon**

Silver service provided by waiters

Turkish delight

The Turkish baths contained hot, medium, and cool rooms; a shampooing room; and a massage couch; as well as a plunge pool in which to cool off. The baths, like the gymnasium, had separate sessions for men and women.

Turkish baths reserved for first-class passengers

👁 EYEWITNESS

The Astors
The wealthiest passenger on board, Colonel John Jacob Astor IV was traveling with his second wife, Madeleine. After the ship struck the iceberg, he helped her into a lifeboat, reportedly saying, "You'll be alright ... I'll see you in the morning." He did not survive.

Second class

Dining in style
This plate from the second-class service shows the strict class structure on board. Each class ate from a different style of plate.

On board the *Titanic*, the second-class facilities were far superior to the first-class facilities of most rival liners. The oak-paneled dining saloon provided a four-course dinner followed by fruit, cheese, and coffee. Passengers had use of a library, a barber's shop, and a range of bars and saloons. The cabins were comfortable, and the open decks provided space for games and relaxation.

Father and daughter
This photograph shows second-class passengers Robert Phillips and his daughter, Alice, who boarded the *Titanic* at Southampton. Alice survived the disaster, but tragically her father was lost.

👁 EYEWITNESS

Letter home
During the stop in Ireland on April 11, many passengers mailed letters home describing life on board. The writer of this letter reports, "we have been having very rough weather," although the first overnight passage was in fact quite calm.

Passengers dwarfed by huge funnels

On deck
The boat deck had plenty of space to relax. A safer ship would have had less room, however, as the deck area would have held extra lifeboats.

Traveling rug to keep out the cold

In the hold

All luggage not needed during the voyage was stored in the hold. Second-class passengers may not have had as much luggage as those in first class, but they would all have traveled with evening wear for dinner.

Second-class label for luggage to be stored in the hold

The Hart family

Benjamin Hart was emigrating to Canada with his wife, Esther, and daughter, Eva. Esther thought the idea of the *Titanic* being "unsinkable" was "flying in the face of God." Convinced of disaster, she slept during the day and kept watch at night. Eva and her mother survived the tragedy, but sadly Benjamin died.

> **"No effort had been spared to give even second-cabin passengers ... the best dinner that money could buy."**
> **—A passenger**

Basin for washing and shaving

Bunked up

Outfitted with mahogany furniture, the 207 second-class cabins were more than comfortable. Located on D, E, F, and G decks, the cabins slept two to four passengers in single beds or bunks.

Wooden seat

White Star Line playing cards

Iron legs

Games of risk

Playing cards was a popular pastime on board. But gambling was risky; professional cheats, traveling under assumed names, hoped to collect big winnings from unsuspecting players.

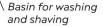

In a spin

In the dining saloon, passengers sat on swivel chairs affixed to the floor. Although the food was prepared in the same kitchen as the first-class meals, the second-class menu was simpler—but no less filling.

Third class

Durable matches
This box of matches bearing the White Star Line logo was recovered from the seabed.

More than half of the total 1,324 passengers—710 in all—were traveling steerage (third class). These passengers came from all over Europe and most were leaving to start a new life in America. More than 100 of the steerage passengers were Irish. Many had never been to sea before, few had any belongings, and all were leaving home with mixed feelings. On board, 220 cabins housed families, while single people were separated—women in cabins at the rear, and men in a large dormitory in the bow.

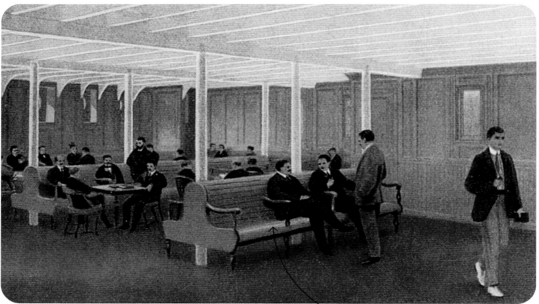

"We were emigrants ... going to Kansas, my father was going to buy a tobacconist's shop."
—Millvina Dean, *Titanic* survivor

Hard-wearing benches of slatted teak

The general room
Paneled with pine and furnished with sturdy benches, tables, and chairs, the general room—the third-class equivalent of a lounge—and the smoking room were the only public rooms available to third-class passengers.

Leather hold-all recovered from the wreck site and restored

Life in a bag
Unlike those in first and second class, most passengers in third class traveled light, having only a few valuables and personal belongings.

Open deck

Buffeted by the wind and blasted by smoke from the ship's funnels, the rear decks allocated to the third-class passengers nevertheless provided a welcome change from the crowded cabins and dining rooms below.

Shift work

Because the dining saloon had space for only 473 people, third-class passengers ate in shifts. Dining tickets showed the times of the sittings.

Inspection card

Each emigrant was issued with a green inspection card stating the place of departure and the holder's last country of residence. Thomas Theobald's inspection card (left) shows that he was transferred from the *Adriatic* to the *Titanic*—a move that cost him his life.

Dining saloon

Four-berth cabin

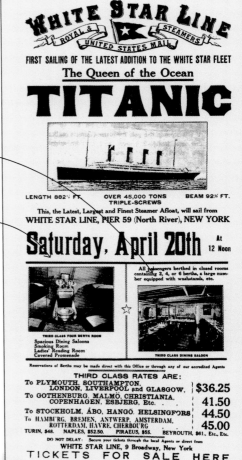

The Goodwin family

Frederick and Augusta Goodwin and their six children, including baby Sidney (not shown here), were emigrating from London to America. None of them survived.

Two months' pay

This advertisement for the voyage that never happened—the return of the *Titanic* to England—gives a good idea as to the cost of a third-class ticket. At $36.25 (£7.46), the price was equivalent to about two months' wages for most third-class passengers.

Atlantic crossing

As the *Titanic* sped across the North Atlantic on Sunday, April 14, 1912, it received a series of messages from other ships in the area, warning of ice. Captain Smith firmly believed that his ship was in no danger, and was urged on by Bruce Ismay, the ship's owner, to prove the vessel's speed and reliability by arriving ahead of schedule.

Titanic illuminations
At night, the *Titanic* shone brightly as the cabin lights glowed and the decks were lit up.

Two clocks show the time at the ship's location and at its destination

Battery charging panel

Wireless room
The use of wireless radio on board ship was still a novelty at that time. Until the *Titanic* disaster, few people realized the importance of radio as a form of emergency communication.

Magnetic detector, or "Maggie"

10" spark transmitter

Headphones for hearing incoming messages

Morse code keys for sending messages

Telegraph message pad

MARCONI WIRELESS TELEGRAPH Co. AMERICA
COMMERCIAL MESSAGES RECEIVED HERE

Transmitter tuning coil

Fleming valve tuner

Marconi telegraph codes book

Multiple tuner for receiving Morse code signals

Wireless operator's logbook

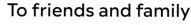

Marconi wireless operators
The *Titanic*'s two wireless operators, Jack Phillips and Harold Bride (right), were employed by Marconi rather than the White Star Line. Bride was only 22 years old, and was paid about £12.50 ($25) a month to work the night shift while his senior colleague, Phillips, rested.

To friends and family
Although most passengers communicated with family and friends by mail, many wealthy passengers used the *Titanic*'s telegraph. Jack Phillips was so busy clearing the backlog of messages that he interrupted the final ice warning from the *Californian* in order to continue transmitting.

> "Captain, *Titanic*: Westbound steamers report **bergs, growlers, and field ice** in 42°N from 49° to 51°W, April 12."
> —Telegraph from Captain Barr of the *Caronia*

HIDDEN DANGER

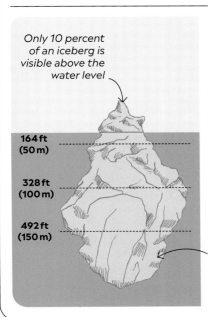

Only 10 percent of an iceberg is visible above the water level

164 ft (50 m)

328 ft (100 m)

492 ft (150 m)

Often, 90 percent of an iceberg's bulk is hidden beneath the sea. Icebergs are formed when chunks of freshwater ice break away from glaciers and float into the sea. They can be up to 150 miles (240 km) long and 70 miles (110 km) wide although smaller "growlers" are also common.

Beneath the sea's surface, an iceberg is bulky, with many sharp edges capable of puncturing a ship's hull

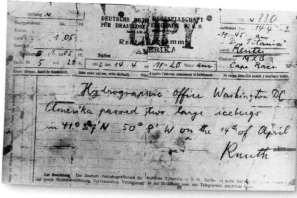

Warning message

As the *Titanic* steamed ahead, it received nine messages warning of ice. Although not all of the warnings reached the bridge, the message from the German ship *Amerika* (above) was passed to Captain Smith in person.

Journey of an iceberg

The icebergs of the North Atlantic begin life in the glaciers of the polar icecap and are carried south by the Labrador Sea, between Canada and Greenland. Some are so large that they survive at sea for several years before melting in warmer waters. In April 1912, the month the *Titanic* sank, 395 icebergs were recorded in the North Atlantic Ocean.

Icebergs can tower above the sea like mountains, or lie flat on the water like frozen fields

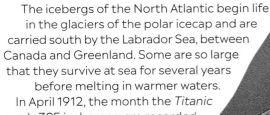

A deadly collision

The night of April 14, 1912, was clear and bitterly cold on the North Atlantic Ocean. The sea was calm and still. Because it was so clear, everyone thought there would be plenty of time to avoid any obstacles. But large ships at full speed do not turn quickly or easily, and when lookout Frederick Fleet spotted an iceberg, at about 11:40 pm, it was too late to avoid a collision.

Warning bell is 17in (43cm) in diameter

Emergency bell
As the iceberg loomed, Fleet struck the crow's nest bell three times—the signal for danger ahead. He also telephoned the bridge.

Mast light indicated the ship's direction of travel

Missing keys
David Blair, one of the crew who sailed the *Titanic* down from Belfast, was not hired for the ship's maiden voyage. In his rush to pack, he left the ship with the keys to the crow's nest telephone still in his pocket.

On board, few of the passengers felt anything more than a slight judder

> ### "It was as though we went over about **a thousand marbles.**"
> —Mrs. Stuart J. White, *Titanic* passenger

Out of sight
The *Titanic* struck the iceberg on the starboard (right) side of its hull. The crew could see only slight damage to the upper decks. However, below the waterline, the iceberg had punched a series of holes along 250 ft (76m) of the hull.

👁 EYEWITNESS

On the lookout
Frederick Fleet was the first to spot the iceberg from the crow's nest. He shouted, "Iceberg, right ahead!," but thought the ship had only a "close shave" rather than a direct hit. Later, he described the iceberg as being "as large as two tables put together."

On the bridge

Although the bridge is the command center of a ship, only four officers were on the *Titanic*'s bridge at the moment of impact. One officer had gone into the officers' quarters, and Captain Smith was in his cabin. Three of these six officers lost their lives in the tragedy.

Open section of bridge from which Murdoch observed the iceberg, seconds after the warning from the lookout

Wheel was linked to the steering mechanism in the stern above the rudder

At the wheel

Quartermaster Robert Hichens turned the wheel hard to starboard (right), swinging the bow to the port (left) of the iceberg. That was all he had time to do.

First Officer Murdoch

William Murdoch was in charge of the bridge at the time of the impact. He ordered the change of direction, and closed the watertight doors. Later, he called all the passengers up on deck to evacuate the ship.

To the lifeboats

At 12:05 am, 25 minutes after the collision, Captain Smith ordered the lifeboats to be uncovered. For the next two hours, total confusion reigned; there had been no lifeboat drill since leaving Southampton, and no one knew what to do. Not one officer realized that the lifeboats could be lowered fully laden. Had they done so, a total of 1,178 people could have been saved, rather than 706.

Women and children first?

The rule on board all ships at that time was to save women and children first. But some men did escape; in many lifeboats, "first come, first saved" was the rule.

EYEWITNESS

Thomas Andrews

Managing director of Harland and Wolff and designer of the *Titanic*, Thomas Andrews had suggested adding more lifeboats to the ship. The idea was rejected to keep the upper deck uncluttered. After the collision, he assessed the damage to the ship and advised passengers to evacuate.

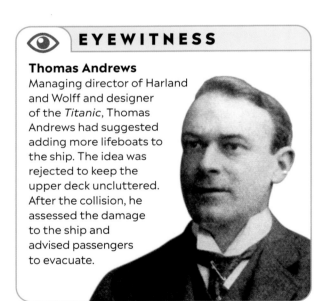

Cork floats covered with thick canvas

Buoyancy aid

Life jackets were available for every passenger and crew member. The life jackets were buoyant enough to keep a person afloat, but they were very bulky to wear and offered little protection against the extreme cold.

> "As I was put into the boat, he (Mr. Daniel Marvin) cried to me,
> ### 'It's all right, little girl. You go. I will stay.' ... "
> —*Titanic* honeymooner
> Mrs. Daniel Marvin

In distress

As the lifeboats filled up, the two radio operators tirelessly sent out distress messages asking for help. Among the ships that picked up the *Titanic*'s pleas were the *Olympic*, the *Baltic*, and the *Carpathia*.

One by one

The lifeboats were lowered starting with number 7 (see below) at 12:45 am, and finishing with collapsible D at 2:05 am. The last two collapsibles floated away from the ship as it sank. The total capacity of all 20 boats was 1,178; it was claimed that about 862 people got into lifeboats. However, according to the US Senate report, only 706 people were saved, which suggests that some people exaggerated the numbers in each boat knowing they had left people to drown.

The collapsibles
Two collapsible lifeboats were stored on deck, and the other two were stowed on the roof of the officers' quarters. The collapsibles had flat, double-bottomed floors and canvas-topped sides, which could be pulled up.

Lifeboat 12 (1:25 am)
Capacity: 65
40 women and children, 2 crew

Lifeboat 14 (1:30 am)
Capacity: 65
53 women, 2 men, 8 crew

Lifeboat 16 (1:40 am)
Capacity: 65
49 women, 1 man, 6 crew

Lifeboat 10 (1:20 am)
Capacity: 65
48 women and children, 2 men, 5 crew

Lifeboat 6 (12:55 am)
Capacity: 65
26 women, 2 crew

Lifeboat 8 (1:10 am)
Capacity: 65
28 women, 4 crew

Lifeboat 4 (1:55 am)
Capacity: 65
35 women and children, 1 man, 4 crew

Lifeboat 2 (1:45 am)
Capacity: 40
21 women, 1 man, 4 crew

Collapsible D (2:05 am)
Capacity: 47
40 women and children, 3 men, 3 crew

Collapsible B (2:20 am)
Capacity: 47
Floated upside down with about 30 men clinging to it

Lifeboat 15 (1:35 am)
Capacity: 65
57 passengers, 13 crew

Lifeboat 13 (1:35 am)
Capacity: 65
55 women and children, 4 men, 5 crew

Lifeboat 11 (1:25 am)
Capacity: 65
60 women and children, 1 man, 9 crew

Lifeboat 9 (1:20 am)
Capacity: 65
42 women, 6 men, 8 crew

Lifeboat 7 (12:45 am)
Capacity: 65
8 women, 10 men, 3 crew

Lifeboat 5 (12:55 am)
Capacity: 65
41 passengers, 1 crew

Lifeboat 3 (1:05 am)
Capacity: 65
25 women and children, 10 men, 15 crew

Collapsible A (2:20 am)
Capacity: 47
Floated off as the ship sank 1 woman, 10 men, 5 crew

Collapsible C (1:40 am)
Capacity: 47
31 women and children, 6 men, 6 crew

Lifeboat 1 (1:10 am)
Capacity: 40
2 women, 3 men, 7 crew

Sir Cosmo　　*Lady Duff Gordon*

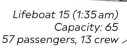

Near collision
Lifeboats 13 and 15 were lowered at the same time. Number 13 reached the water first, but drifted into the path of number 15. The crew had to quickly suspend boat 15 in mid-air until 13 floated away.

Self-help
Some of the people who failed to board a lifeboat tried to build their own rafts out of deckchairs or other buoyant items. Those flung into the sea tried desperately to scramble onto floating wreckage.

Empty vessel
Lifeboat number 1 had only 12 occupants including Sir Cosmo and Lady Duff Gordon. Some people believed they had used their wealth to secure their own lifeboat and crew.

Slowly sinking

As the lifeboats were lowered, there was a flurry of activity on deck. The radio operators sent out distress signals. Officers on the bridge flashed messages by Morse signal lamp and fired rockets to attract the attention of passing ships. Many passengers couldn't believe that the *Titanic* would sink. Some reconciled themselves to their fate, but most believed that help would arrive before the ship went down.

Signaling

Shortly before the first rocket signal was fired, Captain Smith and Fourth Officer Boxhall spotted the lights of a nearby ship. Boxhall flashed the CQD ("come quick, danger") distress signal, but the ship did not respond. New evidence suggests that the ship may have been illegally hunting seals.

Signaling lamp

Rocket signals explode in the sky

> ## "It's the new call, and it might be **your last chance to send it."**
> **—Junior wireless operator, Harold Bride, to Jack Phillips**

The film A Night To Remember *(1958) portrayed the panic-stricken passengers in lifeboats*

Desperation

As the last lifeboats were lowered, several people tried to get into them by sliding down the ropes or leaping from the lower decks. Others jumped into the sea, hoping to climb aboard later. A few lucky people managed to hide in a lifeboat on deck and were only detected once afloat.

The ship's power went out only when it sank, as the engineers stayed behind to keep the electricity and radio running

A gentleman

Once the last lifeboat had left, millionaire Benjamin Guggenheim lost all hope of being saved. He returned to his cabin, where he and his personal attendant changed into evening suits. Before the ship was lost he was heard saying, "We've dressed in our best and are prepared to go down like gentlemen."

Jack Phillips
At first, wireless operator Jack Phillips sent out CQD signals. Then at 12:45 am he sent the new SOS signal—the first ever to be sent from a ship in danger. He sent distress signals tirelessly until the ship lost power.

Final radio message sent by the Titanic

CQD = SOS

The first radio distress signal was CQD. In 1906, the SOS signal was created as the letters were easy to transmit by Morse code. But until the *Titanic* disaster, most Marconi operators still used the old signal.

Key is pressed to tap out messages in Morse code

Morse code
SOS

Morse code
CQD

Communicating in code

Morse code was invented by Samuel Morse in 1838. Each letter is represented as a series of short or long radio signals or flashes of light.

Lights still illuminate the Titanic to draw the attention of any passing ships

Lighting up the sky

Fourth Officer Boxhall fired the first of about eight rocket distress signals at 12:45 am. Each signal—sent up at five-minute intervals—soared 800 ft (244 m) into the air before exploding into a shower of light. Distress signals were always fired at regular intervals so that passing ships would not mistake them for firework displays.

Stern rises high out of the water

The final moments

Kate Winslet and Leonardo DiCaprio in the 1997 film *Titanic*

As the *Titanic* slipped lower into the water, those left on board either tried to make rafts from deckchairs and other items of furniture, or prayed for rescue and comforted their loved ones. As the ship plunged deeper into the sea, the stern rose up in the air, causing a wave of passengers to fall off the deck. Out on the ocean, those lucky survivors in the lifeboats looked away as the *Titanic* met its horrific end.

Against the tide

At about 2:15 am, water crashed through the glass dome at the top of the grand staircase.

Titanic's stern rose up vertically for about 30 seconds before disappearing beneath the sea

Funnels and other equipment on deck broke free and crashed beneath the waves

👁 EYEWITNESS

In time of need
As the ship sank, Father Thomas Byles, a Roman Catholic priest, heard confessions and led prayers at the stern end of the boat deck. Like many of his flock, he lost his life.

Last moments

At 2:18 am, the *Titanic*'s lights went out. The ship was almost vertical, its bow pointing toward the seabed. The ship snapped between the back two funnels, causing the stern section to break free before it also began to sink. At 2:20 am, the *Titanic* finally slipped from view.

Officer Lightoller fires warning shots in the film A Night to Remember (1958)

Panic stations

In case of serious disturbances on board, pistols were kept in a safe for use by senior officers. As the lifeboats were launched, gunshots were fired into the air to prevent panicking crowds from swamping the boats.

All alone

The passengers on the lifeboats must have felt very alone in the dark. Many took turns to row to keep their spirits up and to stay warm.

Propeller and rudder high up in the air

Lifeboats rowed clear of the ship to avoid being dragged down by the ship's suction

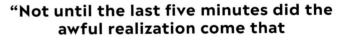

👁 EYEWITNESS

Blasted to safety
Colonel Archibald Gracie was dragged under water by suction from the sinking ship. Then suddenly he was blown clear by a gust of air from a ventilation shaft, and managed to climb onto collapsible lifeboat B. He later detailed his experience in *The Truth About the Titanic* published in 1913.

"Not until the last five minutes did the awful realization come that

the end was at hand.

The lights became dim and went out ... Slowly, ever so slowly, the surface of the water seemed to come up toward us."
—Robert Daniel, passenger

Heroic acts

The extreme dangers that the passengers and crew faced led to some remarkable acts of heroism. Down in the boiler rooms, the firemen and stokers worked until the end to keep the lights burning to attract any passing ships. Up on deck, the two wireless operators sent out distress signals for as long as possible. And all the time the band played on.

Countess of Rothes

In Lifeboat 8, the Countess of Rothes took her turn at the oars before handling the tiller for most of the night. She was later presented with the lifeboat number plate mounted on a plaque.

Molly Brown

US millionairess Molly Brown was one of 26 women on board Lifeboat 6. In charge was Quartermaster Hichens, who refused to let the women row; so Molly Brown took command and rowed furiously toward the rescue ship.

Captain Smith is shown here swimming toward Lifeboat B

Captain Smith

The last minutes of Captain Smith's life are largely uncertain because he went down with his ship. Several survivors claimed that he swam close to the upturned collapsible Lifeboat B, but turned away when he realized how overcrowded its hull was.

Statue of Nike, the Greek goddess of victory

Names of 38 engineers lost with the Titanic

In memoriam

The town most affected by the disaster was Southampton, England, where most of the crew lived. On April 22, 1914, a monument to the ship's engineers was unveiled in the city's East Park. A year later, a smaller memorial to the stewards was unveiled on Southampton Common.

And the band played on

The *Titanic* had two bands—a string quintet, led by violinist Wally Hartley, and a string and piano trio that played outside the à la carte restaurant. After the collision, the musicians gathered in the first-class lounge and played a selection of popular songs to keep the passengers' spirits up. They played on until the very end, going down with their ship.

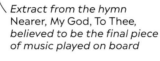

Extract from the hymn *Nearer, My God, To Thee,* believed to be the final piece of music played on board

Engineer at work

Onshore help

New York City mayor William Gaynor (1849–1913) ensured large funds were collected to help the survivors. He wrote letters to people who could help, and organized a Red Cross committee to distribute aid to those in need. Sympathetic to their grief, he urged the press not to bother the "unfortunate people."

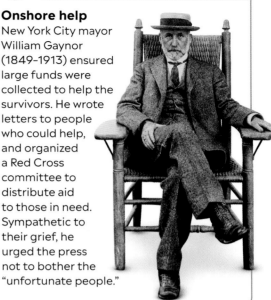

Together forever

Wealthy passenger Isidor Straus was the founder of the famous Macy's department store in New York. Because of his age, he was offered the chance to board a lifeboat, but turned it down. His wife, Ida, refused to leave the ship without him.

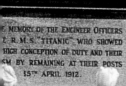

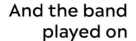

Racing to the rescue

At 12:25 am, the wireless operator on board RMS *Carpathia* picked up a distress message from the *Titanic*. The ship, en route from New York to the Mediterranean, turned around immediately and sailed 58 miles (93 km) northwest to the distressed liner. Captain Rostron prepared his ship to receive survivors. Doctors were put on standby, stewards and cooks prepared accommodation and food, and rockets were fired every 15 minutes to signal the ship's approach.

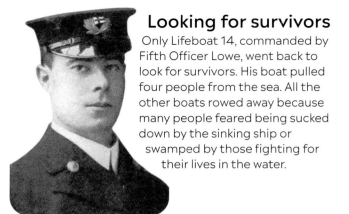

Looking for survivors
Only Lifeboat 14, commanded by Fifth Officer Lowe, went back to look for survivors. His boat pulled four people from the sea. All the other boats rowed away because many people feared being sucked down by the sinking ship or swamped by those fighting for their lives in the water.

Ruth Becker
Separated from her mother, brother, and sister, 12-year-old Ruth Becker still comforted another mother who was separated from her child. Both were reunited with their families aboard the *Carpathia*. Ruth gathered courage for another sea voyage decades later, in 1990.

Smoke spewed from Carpathia's funnel as the ship raced to rescue Titanic's survivors

In sight
At 4:00 am, the *Carpathia* reached the *Titanic*'s last reported position and cut its engines. A green light flickered from Lifeboat 2, where Fourth Officer Boxhall was in charge. Once on board the *Carpathia*, he confirmed the worst to Captain Rostron.

Rowing to safety
The ice field surrounding the survivors meant that it was too dangerous for the *Carpathia* to move in too close. So the exhausted survivors had to row toward the stationary ship. It took four hours to rescue all the survivors.

Masthead lights told survivors that help was on its way

Survivors burned paper and waved their hands to attract attention

Lifeboats hidden among the floating ice

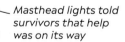

Safe at last

The first survivor, Elizabeth Allen, clambered up a rope ladder to board the *Carpathia* at 4:10 am, just under two hours after the *Titanic* sank. Some survivors had to be winched to safety in a wooden seat.

Gangway door open to receive survivors

Survivors await their turn to board the Carpathia

"After we were picked up on the *Carpathia* my mother came to me ... and said **'You've lost your father, you won't see your father any more ... he's gone.'"**
—Edith Haisman

All hands on deck

As the survivors clambered on board the *Carpathia*, they were met by passengers and crew offering blankets and hot food and drinks. Some were taken to cabins; others huddled on the deck and tried to come to terms with what had happened.

Blankets to keep the survivors warm

Thank you

Survivors of the disaster banned together to buy a silver cup for Captain Rostron and 320 medals for his crew. The reverse side of each medal bore the crew member's name and an inscription of thanks.

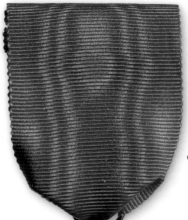

Medal shows the Carpathia sailing through ice

Electric spark

Nicknamed the "electric spark" due to his quick thinking, 42-year-old Captain Arthur Rostron of the *Carpathia* was known for his quick decisions and energetic leadership.

Awaiting news

A young radio enthusiast in New York picked up the *Titanic*'s distress signals early on Monday, April 15. The signals were also detected in Newfoundland, Canada. The word was out that the *Titanic* was in trouble, but other messages during the day appeared to contradict this. It was not until 6:16 pm New York time that it was confirmed that the *Titanic* had sunk.

The worst confirmed

Captain Rostron waited until all the survivors were safely on board before broadcasting any messages. He forwarded a list of survivors, but ignored requests for information from the press until 8:20 pm.

Waiting for news

As news filtered through, concerned relatives arrived at the White Star offices in New York, Southampton, and London (right). It took some days before the first (incomplete) list of survivors was posted in New York.

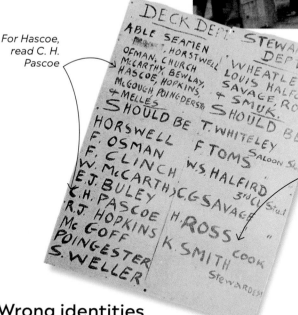

For Hascoe, read C. H. Pascoe

For Ross, read H. Ross, cook

Wrong identities

On Wednesday, a list of saved crew members was posted outside the White Star offices in Southampton, where 699 of the 898 crew lived. In the confusion, names were misspelled and initials missed off, falsely raising some relatives' hopes. Sheets of correct names slowly appeared, finally confirming who had survived.

Read all about it

People started to realize the scale of the disaster from the cries of the newspaper boys. With no firm news from the White Star Line or the rescue ship, *Carpathia*, worried relatives read the newspapers closely, searching for any scrap of information that might tell them about their loved ones.

"I shall pray for the body. He was so good to me."
—*Titanic* survivor writes about her husband

Monday's New York Evening Sun *reported that all passengers were safe*

The Evening Sun.
BASEBALL FINAL EDITION — BASEBALL FINAL EDITION
VOL. XXVI. NO. 25. — NEW YORK, MONDAY, APRIL 15, 1912. — PRICE ONE CENT.

ALL SAVED FROM TITANIC AFTER COLLISION

RESCUE BY CARPATHIA AND PARISIAN;
LINER IS BEING TOWED TO HALIFAX
AFTER SMASHING INTO AN ICEBERG

Baltic, Virginian, Olympic and Other Ships Summoned by Urgent Wireless Calls.

OF LINERS IN CRASH

Over 1,400 Passengers, Many of ——Message from Olympic Telling of Rescue.

GIANTS DROP GAME AT HUB

Boston Braves Win From McGrawites.

THE TITANIC UNDER WAY.

Tuesday morning's Chicago Daily Tribune *confirms the full extent of the horror*

EXTRA **The Chicago Daily Tribune.** EXTRA

LINER TITANIC SINKS; 1300 DROWNED, 866 SAVED

GIANT OF SEA RAMS ICEBERG IN ATLANTIC

THE TITANIC AND ITS CAPTAIN.

Women and Children Saved.

ALGEMEEN HANDELSBLAD van MAANDAG 15 APRIL 1912 – Avondblad – Eerste Blad

DE RAMP VAN DE „TITANIC".

OCHTENDBLAD
Tweede Blad
ONZE OOST.

Although news of the disaster spread rapidly around the world, it did not always make front page news

Around the world

The *Titanic* disaster dominated the newspapers for days, although many of the early stories were often incorrect. Most papers erred on the side of caution, not believing that such a disaster could have happened. Some even printed that the *Titanic* was being towed to Nova Scotia, and that all its passengers were safe.

Good news, bad news

Many women in Southampton lost male relatives in the disaster. Mrs. Rosina Hurst (left) lost her father-in-law, although her husband, fireman Walter Hurst, survived. Sharing the news with her is her aunt, also in mourning clothes.

Lost and found

How many people lost their lives on the *Titanic* will never be known for sure, since the total number of people on board has never been officially established. The US investigation put the total losses at 1,517 (see chart below), while the British inquiry calculated 1,503. But the number of lives tragically lost makes each survivor's story all the more remarkable.

Mrs. Goldsmith wearing two wedding rings

Ring twice

As Mrs. Goldsmith stepped into a lifeboat with her son, family friend Thomas Theobald took off his wedding ring and asked her to pass it on to his wife. Sadly, Mr. Theobald perished.

Honeymooners Mr. and Mrs. Harder

Horrific honeymoons

Eight newlywed couples chose to take their honeymoon on the *Titanic*'s maiden voyage, although only two of the couples lived to tell the tale.

Survivor Mrs. Clara Hays, who lost her husband, Charles Hays, president of Canada's Grand Trunk Railroad

Baby Millvina

Aged only seven weeks at the time of the disaster, Millvina Dean was the youngest survivor of the *Titanic* tragedy. Her mother, Ettie, and brother, Bert, also survived; her father died.

Under cover

Edmond, age 2

Michel, age 3

Louis Hoffmann claimed he was taking his orphaned sons to start a new life in America. In fact, his real name was Michel Navratil and he had left his wife and abducted his sons. The boys survived and were later reunited with their mother.

First class

145 women and children survived, 10 women and 1 child died. Of the men, 54 survived and 119 died. In total, 60% survived.

 199

130

Second class

104 women and children survived, 24 died. Of the men, only 15 survived and 142 died. In total, 42% survived.

119

166

Third class

105 women and children survived, 119 died. Of the men, only 69 survived and 417 died. In total, 25% survived.

174

536

Crew

20 women survived, 3 died. Of the men, 194 survived and 682 died. In total, 24% survived.

 214

Saved

Lost

Table showing how the death toll varied among the three classes and crew

685

Limping home
On arrival in New York, Harold Bride's feet were so frostbitten that he had to be carried ashore. One of the heroes of the disaster, Bride had carried on sending distress signals until minutes before the *Titanic* sank.

Hat removed out of respect for the dead

Harold Bride's ankles were badly injured during the escape, and his feet were frostbitten

Rest in peace
On April 20, less than a week after the disaster, Canon Kenneth Hind held a funeral service on board the *Mackay-Bennett*. Too disfigured to be identified, 24 people were sewn into weighted sacks and given a dignified burial at sea.

Body is pulled from the sea into Mackay-Bennett's rowing boat

Finding bodies
The gruesome task of collecting bodies was carried out by ships from Halifax, Nova Scotia. The *Mackay-Bennett* carried tons of ice to preserve the bodies and more than 100 coffins. Over the next six weeks, 328 bodies were found.

"… the boat was upside down and I was under it … How I got out from under the boat I do not know, but I felt a breath of air at last."

—Harold Bride

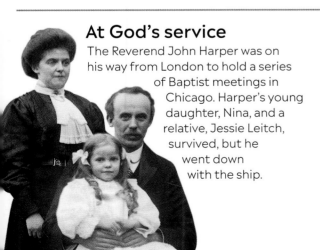

At God's service
The Reverend John Harper was on his way from London to hold a series of Baptist meetings in Chicago. Harper's young daughter, Nina, and a relative, Jessie Leitch, survived, but he went down with the ship.

👁 EYEWITNESS

Writing home
Many survivors wrote letters to friends or family describing their ordeal. Mary Hewlett, who was in Lifeboat 13, wrote, "I had some long letters I had written to my girls … and I gave them to be burned, sheet by sheet, as signals. The dawn came at about 4:30 am … soon after that we saw the mast lights of the *Carpathia* on the horizon."

Lives lost

Every life lost on the *Titanic* was a tragedy. Some of the dead were rich and famous. Many were third-class passengers about to start a new life in America. Servants traveling with their employers and the many men and women who worked on the ship were all caught up in the terrible event. Few of them lived to tell the tale.

Archibald Butt
Archibald Butt was a US army officer and a military aide to President William Taft. Before the race for the presidential elections in November 1912 began, Butt took a six-week holiday in Europe, returning home on the *Titanic*.

Third-class passengers
One-third of the lives lost were third-class passengers, many of whom were crossing the Atlantic to start a new life. Some of them might have achieved great success, but they did not survive to live out their dreams.

John Thayer
John Borland Thayer was an American cricket player, visiting England in 1884 as part of the Philadelphian team. He later became vice-president of the Pennsylvania Railroad. In 1912, he and his family went to Europe, coming back on the *Titanic*.

Passengers boarding the *Titanic*

Remembering the dead

Crew members of the US Coast Guard Cutter *Juniper* scattered 1.5 million dried rose petals over the resting site of the *Titanic* in 2012, a hundred years after the tragedy. Commander Lisa Mack said, "Now it's up to us to keep their memory alive ... Icebergs are still a threat to transatlantic mariners."

This baker's hat belonged William E. Hine, who perished in the disaster

The chefs

Only 13 of the 62 people who worked in the *Titanic*'s kitchens survived. The à la carte restaurant was run by restaurant owner Luigi Gatti. All 66 staff were employed by Gatti rather than by the White Star Line. Only three survived. It was later stated that they were locked into their quarters to stop them rushing to the lifeboats.

Servants

Many first-class passengers brought their valets, maids, chauffeurs, cooks, and nannies with them. Few survived, although some did manage to get aboard a lifeboat, including Mary Anne Perrault, the maid to Mrs. Hays.

A still from the German film *Titanic* (1943) showing the ship's engineering crew at work

Below decks

All 25 general engineers, and the 10 engineers who kept the mechanical equipment running, lost their lives. So, too, did 10 of the 13 leading firemen, 53 of the 73 coal trimmers, 118 of the 163 stokers, and 29 of the 33 greasers.

Statue damaged by bombs during World War II

Monument stands 48 ft (14.6 m) tall

Heroes of the Marine Engine Room

A memorial to the "engine room heroes" was erected in Liverpool, England. It was designed by Welsh sculptor Sir William Goscombe John and unveiled on May 6, 1916.

Survival stories

The lives of many of the survivors were totally changed, and not always for the best. Some thanked their rescuers, others were called cowards, and a few got divorced. Some contributed to the publicity surrounding the event; others refused to talk about their ordeal.

Living on
Most survivors tried to put the tragedy behind them. Those who lived long enough had to relive their memories when the wreck of the *Titanic* was found in 1985.

The Carters
Lucile Carter, wife of wealthy American William Carter, became a hero for rowing Lifeboat 4. She believed her husband had drowned, only to find him on board the *Carpathia* the next day. In 1914, the couple divorced, with Lucile accusing her husband of having cruelly deserted her and their children on the *Titanic*.

Madeleine Astor
Madeleine Astor was the pregnant wife of John Jacob Astor IV, who died on the ship. She managed to get into Lifeboat 4 and survived. Later, she cohosted a luncheon in New York for Captain Rostron of the *Carpathia* and Dr. Frank McGee, the ship's doctor, to thank them for their help.

Lifeboat
Not all those who survived enjoyed a happy life. Arthur Peuchen, president of Standard Chemical, Iron & Lumber Co of Canada, offered his services as a yachtsman and was told to go on to Lifeboat 6. He found himself with Molly Brown (see p. 40) and later exaggerated his own role. For surviving and boasting about it, he was heavily criticized and called a coward.

A lifeboat approaches the Carpathia *that came to help*

Millvina Dean

Dean was the youngest survivor of the disaster at only seven weeks old, but lived to be the last-living survivor, dying in 2009 at the age of 97. In later life, she spoke at many *Titanic* events and made several radio and television appearances.

New York City residents gave clothes in this suitcase to Dean's family, who had lost everything

Pets

As well as passengers and crew, there were a large number of cats, dogs, and birds on board. Only three dogs survived: Margaret Hays' Pomeranian in Lifeboat 7, Elizabeth Rothschild's Pomeranian in Lifeboat 6, and Henry Harper's Pekingese in Lifeboat 3.

Edwina looks over a 10 ft (3 m) model of the Titanic

Edwina Troutt

Edwina Troutt was traveling on the *Titanic* to be with her sister in America. Edwina survived to celebrate her 100th birthday before dying in December 1984.

TITANIC

Lessons learned

Life buoy

Four days after the *Titanic* sank, the first official inquiry opened in New York, chaired by Senator William Alden Smith. The 82 witnesses included Bruce Ismay, the White Star chairman; Guglielmo Marconi; lookout Frederick Fleet; and Captain Lord of the *Californian*. Two weeks later, the British inquiry began under Lord Mersey. The US inquiry was led by politicians looking for someone to blame, while the British inquiry was led by lawyers and technical experts trying to establish the facts to ensure there was no repetition of the disaster. Both inquiries called for ships to be safer and built to higher standards.

Titanic survivors line up to receive shipwreck pay

The forgotten crew

Under the White Star Line's conditions, the *Titanic*'s crew ceased to be paid at 2:20 am on April 15, the moment the ship sank. Some received expenses, but most were shipped straight home by White Star with little or no financial aid. Many had to rely on emergency shipwreck pay until they could find another job.

Who was to blame?

The US inquiry blamed Captain Smith because of his "overconfidence and neglect." It also blamed Captain Lord of the *Californian* for not coming to the rescue, and the British Board of Trade for not updating its lifeboat regulations. The British inquiry blamed neither Captain Smith nor the Board of Trade.

Scale model of the Titanic

Sir Cosmo Duff Gordon gives evidence

Presiding judge, Lord Mersey

The British *Titanic* inquiry in progress

Ice patrol

In 1914, 16 North Atlantic nations established the International Ice Patrol to look out for icebergs in the North Atlantic shipping lanes. Nowadays, the patrol uses ships and airplanes with radar, underwater sonar equipment, and the latest forecasting technology to report the location of icebergs to every ship in the area.

More lifeboats

The main recommendation of both inquiries was that every ship be outfitted with enough lifeboats for everyone on board, and that regular lifeboat drills be held. This meant placing more lifeboats on deck, which restricted the passengers' view of the sea.

Lifeboats hang beneath the decks of this modern liner, allowing passengers a clear view across the sea

Guglielmo Marconi, inventor of wireless telegraphy

On air

Both inquiries recommended that every ship be outfitted with a radio and that radio contact be maintained 24 hours a day. They also advised that all ship radios should follow international regulations.

Last of the line

Although the *Titanic* proved that watertight bulkheads could not stop a ship from sinking, the designers of the Italian liner *Andrea Doria* claimed their ship was unsinkable. But after colliding with the *Stockholm* in 1956, the ship sank when only 1 of its 11 compartments flooded. As the bulkhead filled with water, the ship fell to one side, and water poured in above the compartments.

It took several hours for the Andrea Doria *to plunge 240 ft (73 m) beneath the sea*

End of **an era**

The *Titanic* was meant to be the second in a series of three White Star Line luxury liners. Only one of the three—the *Olympic*—lived up to expectations. The *Titanic* sank, and the *Britannic* was only ever used for military service. After the *Titanic* tragedy, the *Olympic* was fitted with extra safety measures and cruised the North Atlantic for more than 20 years as both a civilian and a military ship. In 1935, it sailed its final voyage.

Not so gigantic

The third of the great White Star Liners was originally called the *Gigantic*, but it was renamed *Britannic* to avoid comparisons with the *Titanic*. With the recent tragedy in mind, it was outfitted with enough lifeboats for everyone on board.

Troop ship

During World War I, the *Olympic* became a naval transport ship and, over a three-year period, ferried 119,000 troops and civilians. It survived three submarine attacks, earning itself the nickname "Old Reliable."

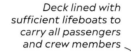

Deck lined with sufficient lifeboats to carry all passengers and crew members

"Dazzle" paint camouflage to confuse enemy submarines

Friends and family wave to passengers aboard the Olympic as it leaves New York

In service

World War I broke out only six months after the *Britannic*'s launch on February 26, 1914. The ship was quickly transformed into a hospital ship, with dormitories and operating theaters on each deck.

Red crosses painted on the side of the hull indicate that the Britannic *is a hospital ship*

The boom years

The *Olympic* returned to civilian service in July 1920. For the next 15 years, the ship carried many thousands of passengers across the Atlantic. The ship had only one major accident, when it struck a lightship in heavy fog in May 1934. Seven of the lightship's 11 crew members were killed. By 1935, the *Olympic* had become dated, and later that year it was sold, stripped of its fittings, and scrapped.

To the seabed

On November 21, 1916, the *Britannic* was sailing northward through the Kea Channel, south of Athens. A sudden explosion ripped the ship open and sank it within an hour. It is thought that the ship struck a mine.

Massive hole ripped out of the Britannic's *port side*

Olympic's shape was sleeker than other ships of the time

Paneling from the first-class à la carte restaurant of the RMS Olympic

Afterlife

Many of the fittings from the *Olympic* were removed from the ship before it was scrapped, and stored in a barn in England. Rediscovered 56 years later, the fittings were offered for sale and now furnish hotels, factories, and homes across England.

Search and discovery

Just after midnight on September 1, 1985, scientists on board *Knorr*, the ship searching for the wreck of the *Titanic*, spotted the wreckage of a boiler on the ship's monitors. The camera followed a trail of objects until, suddenly, the huge black shadow of the *Titanic*'s hull came into view. The *Titanic* had been found 73 years after its tragic loss.

The *Titanic* was located at 41°43'N, 49°56'W, 480 miles (770 km) southeast of Newfoundland, Canada, on a sloping seabed overlooking a canyon.

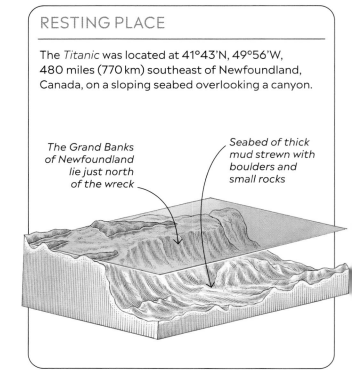

The Grand Banks of Newfoundland lie just north of the wreck

Seabed of thick mud strewn with boulders and small rocks

The wreck

The bow and stern sections of the ship lie 1,970 ft (600 m) apart on the seabed. Both are upright, the bow section having plowed 65 ft (20 m) into the mud.

Peeping into the past

Among the many items picked up from the wreck was one of the ship's portholes. Plates, cutlery, and light fixtures were also scooped up from the sea floor.

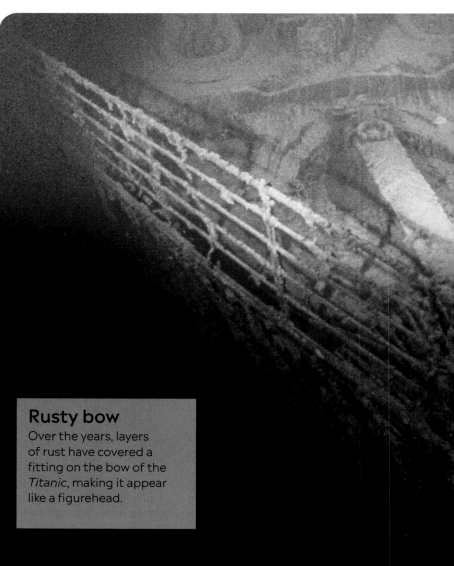

Rusty bow

Over the years, layers of rust have covered a fitting on the bow of the *Titanic*, making it appear like a figurehead.

All aboard

Life on board *Nautile* was cramped and hot. The crew lay on their sides, looking out at the wreck through the small portholes.

Nautile

Picking up the pieces

In July 1987, French scientists sailed to the site of the *Titanic* to carry out investigations. The expedition worked from the surface ship *Nadir* (above), and a crew of three explored the seabed in the submersible *Nautile*. The crew scooped 1,800 objects from the seabed.

Hostile waters

The *Titanic* lies in 12,470 ft (3,800 m) of water. At this depth, there is no light and the temperature is no more than 36°F (2°C).

1,640 ft
(500 m)

3,280 ft
(1,000 m)

Gigantic boilers

As the ship sank, 5 of its 29 vast boilers broke completely free of the ship and were later found in the field of debris.

6,561 ft
(2,000 m)

9,842 ft
(3,000 m)

Toppled telegraph

This telegraph from the docking bridge was used to communicate with the engine room when maneuvering the ship in and out of port.

13,123 ft
(4,000 m)

Treasure trove

Many of the artifacts from the wreck were stored in French laboratories and used to help scientists study the harmful effects of seawater. Most of the artifacts have now been carefully restored.

A collection of well-preserved spoons recovered from the seabed

Objects are washed in fresh water to remove mud and salt

Coals from the seabed

Among the items raised from the seabed are pieces of coal that fell from the bunkers. These lumps of coal are the only artifacts from the wreck to have been sold—to raise funds for future salvage efforts.

A new direction

The ship's compass (right) stood on a wooden stand, much of which was eaten away by marine worms. Conservationists have carefully restored much of the stand.

Fused as one

Seawater produces rust on metal that cements objects into combinations called concretions. Here, spoons and a lump of china have become firmly attached. To separate such objects, conservators pass electricity through the metal objects in a chemical bath, which softens the concretion.

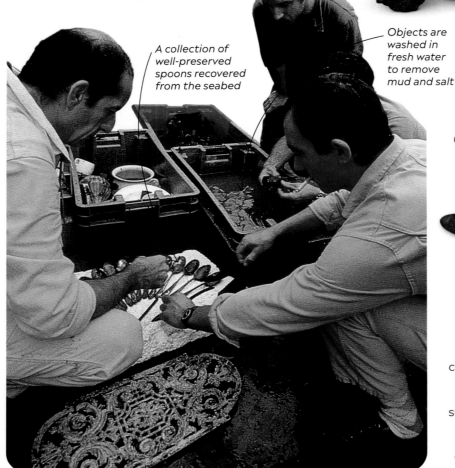

Steel fitting recovered from the wreck site

Missing pieces

The discovery of the *Titanic* wreck and the artifacts rescued from the seabed have solved some of the questions about the fatal voyage. We now know that the hull broke up as it sank, and that the steel used in its construction could not withstand the icy waters of the North Atlantic. The ship sank some 13 miles (21km) away from the position estimated at the time of the disaster, casting doubt on various accounts of which ships were in the area and able to come to the rescue.

Metal fatigue

Examining the steel used in the hull revealed that the plates and rivets became brittle in low water temperatures. On the night of the disaster, the water temperature was about 31°FC (-0.2°). Also, the steel had a high sulfur content, which made it more liable to fracture. This explains why the iceberg caused such serious damage to the hull.

Sliced by ice

It was long thought that the iceberg sliced into the *Titanic*, causing one continuous gash along the hull. Recent sonar images, however, show that the iceberg actually made six narrow holes in the ship's hull.

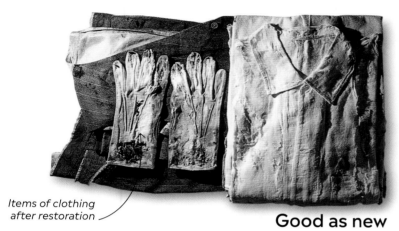

Items of clothing after restoration

Good as new

Many items of clothing from the wreck were remarkably well preserved, having been stored in trunks or drawers. Clothes recovered include a pair of gloves, a pressed shirt, and a steward's jacket.

Hand-clean only

The only way to restore sea-damaged clothes is by hand. With careful brushing and the use of sensitive cleaning materials, the effects of almost 100 years under the sea can slowly be reversed.

Rubber gloves protect hands against the harmful effects of chemicals

Clothes dusted to remove specks of dust and debris

WHAT HAPPENED?

Some eyewitnesses stated that the ship broke in two before it sank; others claimed it went down in one piece. The discovery of the wreck in two pieces, some 1,970 ft (600 m) apart on the seabed, confirms that the hull did indeed break up.

Stage 1
As the "watertight" compartments filled with water, the bow slowly sank, pulling the stern upward and out of the water.

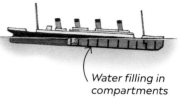

Water filling in compartments

Stage 2
The weight of water inside the hull pulled the bow underwater. By now the stern was right up in the air, causing deck equipment, engines, and internal fittings to break loose.

Stage 3
The keel could stand the strain no more and fractured between the third and fourth funnels.

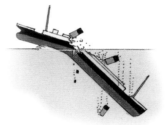

Stage 4
The bow plummeted downward to the seabed. It broke free of the stern section, which floated by itself momentarily before it, too, sank.

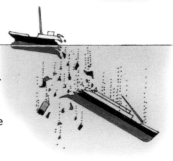

The story continues

With countless films, books, musicals, songs, computer games, and websites to its name, the ill-fated *Titanic* is now more famous than ever. Phrases associated with the ship—"and the band played on" and "tip of the iceberg"—have entered the English language, and there can be few people who do not have some knowledge of this fascinating story. The *Titanic* may lie rusting at the bottom of the Atlantic, but interest in the ship—and the magical era it was a part of—lives on.

Titanic musicals
Based on the larger-than-life character of Molly Brown (p. 40), the musical *The Unsinkable Molly Brown* opened in New York in 1960 and was a great success. The musical *Titanic* (above), staged in 1997, highlighted the great divide between the rich passengers in first class and the poor emigrants in third class.

Supplement to the Sphere Magazine, April 27, 1912

Memorial edition of the Daily Graphic, April 20, 1912

Daily Mirror, April 16, 1912

In print
Within days of the disaster, newspapers were producing memorial editions packed with photographs and artistic reconstructions. Songwriters produced mournful songs, postcard companies printed memorial cards, and publishers produced hastily written books.

Sheet music for The Ship That Will Never Return, *written by F. V. St. Clair*

A drop in the ocean
The film *Raise the Titanic* (1980) was a huge failure. It cost £35 million and made so little money that its producer remarked, "It would have been cheaper to lower the Atlantic."

Sheet music for The Wreck of the Titanic, *written by Haydon Augarde*

The Deathless Story of the Titanic, *issued by Lloyd's Weekly News, 1912*

Walter Lord

Walter Lord's book *A Night To Remember* (1955) was based on interviews with more than 60 survivors of the disaster. The book was televised in 1956 and turned into a successful documentary-style film in 1958.

3D reconstruction

On a 3D *Titanic* video game, you can wander around the ship, explore the public rooms and cabins, stand on deck, and relive the ship's final moments.

EYEWITNESS

Silent star

One survivor to prosper from the tragedy was the American actor Dorothy Gibson, who escaped in one of the lifeboats. A month after the disaster, she starred in a silent movie, *Saved From the Titanic*, wearing the same clothes she had worn when the ship sank. She had a successful film career.

The big time

The film *Titanic*, released in 1997, was one of the most successful films of all time. Directed by James Cameron and starring Kate Winslet and Leonardo DiCaprio, the film won 11 Oscars. Within two years, it had made $1,826 million (£1,141 million) at the box office.

Raise the *Titanic*?

Ever since the ship sank in 1912, plans have been put forward to raise the *Titanic* off the seabed. Suggestions included attaching magnets or bags of helium to the ship's hull. There was even a scheme to fill the ship with ping-pong balls! As the debate over whether to raise the *Titanic* or leave it in peace continues, the rusting wreck continues to disintegrate.

The *Titanic* lives on

A century after the disaster, people continue to be fascinated by the ship's tragic end. Exhibitions of artifacts tour the world, and a new museum has opened in Belfast. New evidence published in 2010 suggests a twist to the story, but the reality is that there will never be a definite answer as to why a brand-new ship should have sunk so quickly.

Seen by millions

Artifacts from the wreck are on display in nine museums in the US and Paris and constantly tour the world. Millions of people visit the exhibitions, which include models of the ship on the seabed.

A model of *Titanic* showing it on the seabed

Brick model

LEGO® designer Ryan McNaught paid tribute to the *Titanic* using 120,000 LEGO® bricks to recreate the sinking of the ship. It took him and his teammates about 250 hours to build the model, which they completed in January 2016.

Reviving Belfast

Titanic Belfast (right), a major museum dedicated to the *Titanic*, opened in 2012 in Belfast, where the ship was built. The building sits on ground previously occupied by the Harland and Wolff shipyard. The area is part of a major scheme to revive Belfast's economy.

Robert Hichens

Some people claim that a steering error caused the tragedy. First Officer Murdoch used the old tiller commands to tell Robert Hichens to steer left. Hichens, however, was used to modern commands and turned the wheel so that the ship turned right, straight into the iceberg.

THE SPHERE

Charles Lightoller

Second Officer Lightoller had to give evidence to both the US and British inquiries. However, he was persuaded by Bruce Ismay to mislead both inquiries because the *Titanic* was inadequately insured. Lightoller kept quiet to save everyone's job.

Bruce Ismay

Chairman of the White Star Line, Bruce Ismay, ordered Captain Smith to keep the *Titanic* moving slowly ahead after the collision. This made it sink far quicker than it otherwise would have done, and led to many unnecessary deaths. As a result of the disaster, his reputation was destroyed and Ismay kept out of the public eye until he died in 1937.

Bruce Ismay giving evidence to the inquiry into the sinking

Angular steel walls recall the ship's prow—the front part that cuts through the water

Louise Patten

Novelist Louise Patten is the granddaughter of Charles Lightoller (above left). In 2010, she published a novel *Good as Gold*, in which she used information passed down from her grandfather to claim that a basic steering error was a main cause of the disaster.

Did you know?

AMAZING FACTS

Loading coal at the docks

The *Titanic* was carrying 6,598 tons (5,986 metric tons) of coal.

Richard Norris Williams refused to have his legs amputated after being rescued from the *Titanic*. He went on to fully recover and won an Olympic gold medal for tennis in 1924.

Containers of biscuits and water were stowed in the lifeboats, but the survivors did not know they were there.

There were at least nine dogs on board the ship. Three of the dogs survived.

Harland and Wolff employed more than 15,000 workmen to build the *Olympic* and the *Titanic*.

There was a 50-phone switchboard on the *Titanic*. The crew, and some first-class passengers, could talk to each other, but it was not possible to speak to people on land.

There were only two bathtubs on board for more than 700 third-class passengers.

Harland and Wolff workmen tightening bolts

Richard Norris Williams

The lights were working on the *Titanic* until two minutes before it sank.

The cheapest third-class fare on the *Titanic* was £7.75 ($40), including meals. A second-class ticket cost £13 ($60), while a first-class ticket was £30 ($150). Tickets for the promenade suites on B deck cost £870 ($4,350).

A daily newspaper called the *Atlantic Daily Bulletin* was produced on board.

There was a small hole at the bottom of each lifeboat to ensure that water did not collect in the boat while on deck. Lifeboat 5 had reached the water before its hole was blocked.

Ostrich feather

Chief Baker, Charles Joughin, was standing on the stern as the ship sank; he was able to just step into the water. He survived in the freezing ocean for two hours until, eventually, survivors managed to pull him into Lifeboat 12.

Among the goods transported by the *Titanic* were 12 cases of ostrich plumes.

You can smell icebergs before you see them! Minerals give off a distinct smell as the ice melts.

The original plans allowed room for 64 lifeboats. However, the owners and builders of the *Titanic* reduced the number to 16 in order to provide more space for passengers on the boat deck. They added four lifeboats with collapsible sides.

QUESTIONS AND ANSWERS

Why were third-class passengers given a medical check on boarding?

Being emigrants, third-class passengers were given a medical check to make sure they were healthy to enter the US.

What are growlers?

Slabs of ice broken away from icebergs are known as growlers.

What were the *Titanic*'s two masts used for?

A crane on the foremast lifted cars and heavy goods. A ladder inside the foremast led up to the crow's nest. Wires stretched between the two formed part of the wireless communication system.

How many lifeboats are there on ships today?

Modern cruise ships have enough lifeboats for 25 percent more people than they should have on board.

There is no smoke from the fourth funnel.

On finding the *Titanic*'s hull, what did explorers see on the foremast?

The foremast collapsed across the deck and the crow's nest was seen.

What happened to sick people on the *Titanic*?

There was a hospital with two doctors.

Why did the *Titanic* have four funnels?

The *Titanic*'s owners thought four funnels would look better than three.

Why didn't the lookouts use binoculars?

Lookouts Frederick Fleet and Reginald Lee thought the binoculars were left in Southampton.

Why was the *Titanic*'s maiden voyage delayed from March 20 to April 10, 1912?

When the *Olympic* collided with HMS *Hawke* in September 1911, work was stopped on the *Titanic* to repair the hole in *Olympic*'s side.

The bow of the *Titanic* on the seabed

RECORD BREAKERS

- In 1912, the *Olympic* and the *Titanic* were the largest ships in the world.

- The *Titanic* was the largest human-made object that had ever been moved, measuring 882 ft 9 in (269.1 m) long and 92 ft 6 in (28 m) wide.

- The two parlor suites on B deck were the most beautifully decorated staterooms on any ocean liner.

- To build the *Olympic* and the *Titanic*, Harland and Wolff constructed a huge metal framework, called a gantry. It was the largest gantry in the world.

A contemporary postcard comparing the *Titanic* to the world's tallest buildings

Timeline

The building of the RMS *Titanic* and her tragic loss is a story that has fascinated thousands of people over the last century. This timeline sets out the key points, from the initial idea of the liner; through its design, construction, and launch; to the fatal collision with the iceberg; the sinking; and finally, many decades later, the discovery of the wreck.

The construction of the *Titanic*

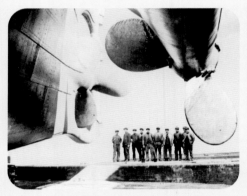
Two of the *Titanic*'s huge propellers

Summer 1907
Lord Pirrie, chairman of Harland and Wolff, and Bruce Ismay, director of the White Star Line, decide to build three huge, luxurious liners called *Olympic*, *Titanic*, and *Britannic*.

March 31, 1909
Construction of the *Titanic* begins.

May 31, 1911
The *Titanic* is launched.

May 31, 1912
Outfitting is complete and the *Titanic* is ready to sail.

April 2, 1912
Tugs pull the *Titanic* out to sea for her sea trials.

8:00 pm The *Titanic* leaves Belfast for Southampton.

April 3, 1912
The *Titanic* arrives in Southampton.

April 4–10 ,1912
Last-minute painting and the outfitting of furniture and carpets; the hiring of the crew; loading coal, cargo, and provisions for the trip.

Wednesday, April 10, 1912
6:00 am Crew board *Titanic*.
7:30 am Captain Smith boards.
9:30 am Bruce Ismay arrives. He will stay in one of the parlor suites with a private promenade deck.
9:30–11:30 am Passengers board.
Noon *Titanic* finally sets sail for France, but is slightly delayed by the near collision with the *New York*.
6:35 pm *Titanic* drops anchor in Cherbourg harbor. Two small White Star steamships bring passengers, luggage, and mail out to the *Titanic*.
8:10 pm *Titanic* sets off for Ireland.

Thursday, April 11
11:30 am *Titanic* arrives at Queenstown and anchors 2 miles (3 km) offshore.
1:30 pm *Titanic* leaves Queenstown and sets sail for New York.

Third-class daily menu

Friday, April 12
Titanic receives wireless messages of congratulations on the maiden voyage and also warning that there is ice in the sea-lanes. Captain Smith steers farther south.

Saturday, April 13
11:00 pm The wireless machine stops working. Jack Phillips and his assistant Harold Bride work all night and repair it by 5:00 am.

Sunday, April 14
9:00 am *Titanic* receives ice warnings from the *Caronia*.
11:40 am Liner *Noordam* reports ice.
1:42 pm White Star Liner *Baltic* warns of icebergs and field ice. Captain Smith shows this warning to Bruce Ismay.
1:45 pm German liner *Amerika* reports two large icebergs. This message fails to reach Captain Smith.
7:30 pm Harold Bride overhears an ice warning from the *Californian* and sends it to the bridge.
9:30 pm Second Officer Lightoller instructs the lookouts to watch for ice.
9:30 pm The *Mesaba* warns of large icebergs. Jack Phillips is busy and does not send the warning to the bridge.

Titanic leaves Queenstown (now known as Cobh)

10:55 pm Jack Phillips, exhausted, cuts off the *Californian*'s ice warning.
11:40 pm Lookout Frederick Fleet sees the iceberg. First Officer Murdoch orders the engine room to stop the engines, tells Quartermaster Hichens to turn "hard a'starboard" (left), and closes the doors between the watertight compartments.
11:40 pm The *Titanic* hits the iceberg, only 37 seconds after Fleet's warning.
11:41 pm Captain Smith instructs Fourth Officer Boxhall to inspect the ship for damage.
11:50 pm Thomas Andrews inspects the damaged areas.

Harold Bride at work in the radio room

Monday, April 15
Midnight Thomas Andrews tells Captain Smith the ship will sink within 90 minutes.
12:05 am Captain Smith orders the lifeboats to be uncovered.

2:17 am The bow plunges underwater.
2:18 am The *Titanic* breaks into two. The bow section sinks.
2:20 am Two of the collapsible lifeboats wash overboard, one half-flooded, the other upside down.
2:20 am The stern sinks.
4:10 am Survivors from the first lifeboat board the *Carpathia*.
8:10 am Survivors from the last lifeboat board the *Carpathia*.
Noon Reports reach New York that the *Titanic* is still afloat and all are safe.
6:16 pm Captain Haddock of the *Olympic* confirms that the *Titanic* has sunk.

Tuesday, April 16
Carpathia posts a list of survivors at *The New York Times* office.

Wednesday, April 17
The steamer *Mackay-Bennett* leaves Halifax. It searches the area for nine days and finds 306 bodies. Later, steamers find another 22 bodies.

Thursday, April 18
Carpathia reaches New York with 705 survivors.

April 19–May 25
Inquiry into the disaster by the US Senate.

Survivors reach the *Carpathia*

1960
The musical *The Unsinkable Molly Brown* opens.

July 1980, June 1981, July 1983
American Jack Grimm leads three attempts to find the wreck.

September 1, 1985
Robert Ballard's French/US expedition with search ship *Knorr* and uncrewed submersible *Argo* discovers the wreck of the *Titanic*.

July 1986
Robert Ballard photographs the wreck in a submarine called *Alvin*.

July 1987
A salvaging expedition, with search ship *Nadir* and crewed submersible *Nautile*, starts lifting objects from the wreck. Further expeditions in 1993 and 1994 raise more than 5,000 objects.

1991
A Soviet/Canadian expedition films the wreck for a documentary called *Titanica*.

Newspaper headlines about the disaster

December 18, 1997
The film *Titanic* opens in the US.

April 2003
The film *Ghosts of the Abyss* premieres.

The Titanic's propellers rise out of the water

Lifeboats row away as the stern sinks

12:10 am Captain Smith asks Jack Phillips to send out a call for help. The *Olympic*, *Frankfurt*, and *Carpathia* reply.
12:25 am *Carpathia* sets off to help, but is 58 miles (93 km) away.
12:45 am The first lifeboat is lowered.
12:45 am The first distress flare is sent.
About 1:00 am First news reaches the US that the *Titanic* has hit an iceberg.
2:05 am The last lifeboat is lowered.

May 2–July 3
British Board of Trade Inquiry into the disaster.

May 14
Dorothy Gibson, one of the survivors, writes and stars in a silent movie, *Saved From the Titanic*.

July 3, 1958
The film *A Night To Remember* debuts.

The crewed submersible *Nautile*

Find out more

If the story of the *Titanic* has captured your imagination, there are many ways to find out more. There are a number of exhibitions about the *Titanic*, which often include objects from the wreck. You can learn more about the ship by making a model or looking at plans. Watching a movie about the *Titanic* will also help to bring the liner's last tragic journey to life.

Olympic story

By finding out about the *Titanic*'s sister ship, the *Olympic*, you will learn a great deal about the design and style of the *Titanic*.

Sea nymphs hold a drowned sailor

The grand staircase

Organizers of exhibitions about the *Titanic* try to recreate the atmosphere on board and give an idea of the different experiences of first-class, second-class, and third-class passengers. The ornate grand staircase was one of the most striking parts of the *Titanic*'s first-class accommodation.

USEFUL WEBSITES

- To find out about the *Titanic* Historical Society, see: **www.titanichistoricalsociety.org**
- For all sorts of information about the *Titanic*, go to: **www.titanic-titanic.com**
- To find out about individual passengers and crew members, see: **www.encyclopedia-titanica.org**
- For a transcript of the US Senate and British Board of Trade inquiries, go to: **www.titanicinquiry.org**
- To find out about the *Titanic* Belfast museum, see: **www.titanicbelfast.com**

The Belfast Titanic *memorial was unveiled on June 26, 1920*

Remembering the dead

There are many memorials dedicated to people lost on the *Titanic*. In Southampton, UK, there are separate memorials to the engineers, firemen, musicians, and mail carriers who worked on the *Titanic*. In Belfast, Northern Ireland, there is a memorial for the 22 Ulstermen who died in the disaster.

A *Titanic* model

Constructing a model of the *Titanic* will help you understand its incredible size. You will find out where the lifeboats were kept and discover how frightening it was for the people in the lifeboats to be lowered 60 ft (18 m) down to the water.

Deck plans for the White Star Line RMS Titanic

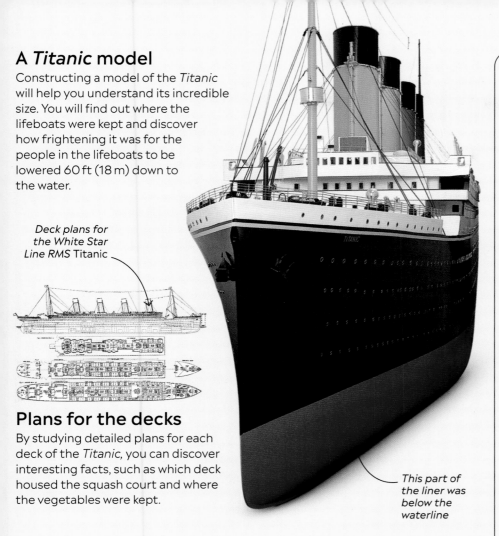

Plans for the decks

By studying detailed plans for each deck of the *Titanic,* you can discover interesting facts, such as which deck housed the squash court and where the vegetables were kept.

This part of the liner was below the waterline

Ghosts of the Abyss

If you want to find out more about the *Titanic* wreck, you need to see the 2003 film *Ghosts of the Abyss*, by James Cameron, director of *Titanic*. Using digital 3D technology, it takes you on an amazing expedition down to the seabed for a trip around the wreck.

Photo from the 1987 Titanic expedition

PLACES TO VISIT

TITANIC BELFAST, BELFAST, NORTHERN IRELAND
• A brand-new museum with nine galleries packed with artifacts, archive material, and full-scale reconstructions. The museum is built on the site of the former Harland and Wolff shipyard where the *Titanic* was built.

MERSEYSIDE MARITIME MUSEUM, LIVERPOOL
• A display focusing on the luxury of the *Titanic* and on the role of these liners in emigration.

NATIONAL MARITIME MUSEUM, LONDON
• A display containing artifacts from the *Titanic*.

SOUTHAMPTON MARITIME MUSEUM, SOUTHAMPTON
• The exhibition tells the story of the *Titanic* through the voices of some of the survivors and the Southampton people whose lives were affected by the disaster.

THE TITANIC MUSEUM, INDIAN ORCHARD, MASSACHUSETTS
• Edward S. Kamuda founded this private museum in 1963 for the survivors of the ship. It contains a unique collection of personal items from survivors, such as letters, postcards, and menus.

MARITIME MUSEUM OF THE ATLANTIC, HALIFAX, CANADA
• The exhibition features artifacts pulled from the water within weeks of the tragedy, including a deckchair and part of the grand staircase.

Medal given to the crew of the *Carpathia*

Finding salvage

Seen here is a robotic arm lifting a masthead lamp from the wreck site. Many of the items found at the site feature in touring exhibitions. It is worth seeking out these collections in order to build a more complete picture of life on board the *Titanic*.

Glossary

AFT At the rear of a ship.

AFT DECK An open deck at the back of the ship for use by third-class passengers.

BERTH A cabin bed or bunk.

BOAT DECK The deck on which the lifeboats are stored.

BOILER A container that heats water to supply steam or heat.

A. M. Carlisle, designer of the *Titanic*, at the British investigation

BOW The front part of the ship.

BRIDGE The control center of the ship.

BULKHEAD The wall in the hold of a ship that can create a watertight compartment.

CABIN An office or living room on a ship.

CLIPPER SHIP A fast sailing ship.

COLLAPSIBLE A lifeboat with canvas sides that collapse for easy storage.

CQD An international Morse code distress call; it was later replaced by SOS.

CREW The people who run a ship. There were 898 on the *Titanic*'s crew list: 875 men and 23 women.

CROW'S NEST A lookout platform high on a ship's mast. On the *Titanic*, the crow's nest was 90 ft (27 m) above the water.

DAVIT A cranelike device outfitted with pulleys and ropes and used to lower lifeboats.

The 1958 film *A Night To Remember*

DRY DOCK A dock that can be pumped dry for work on the bottom of a ship.

ENGINEER A person who helps run the engines and machines.

ENSIGN A flag distinguishing a country or company.

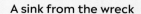

A sink from the wreck

FIREMAN Someone who loads coal into the ship's boilers.

FITTING OUT Installing the decks, machinery, and other equipment inside the empty hull.

FUNNEL A chimney through which smoke from the engines escapes.

FURNACES An enclosed chamber in which coal burns to produce heat.

GANGWAY A passageway into a ship.

GENERAL ROOM A public room like a lounge for the third-class passengers.

GRAND STAIRCASE The staircase connecting the first-class dining saloon with the first-class promenade deck.

GREASER A person who attends to a ship's engines.

HOLD The space for storing cargo.

HULL The main body of a ship.

ICE FIELD A large area of ice in the sea.

INSPECTION CARD Carried by emigrants, the card states the person's name, former country of residence, port of departure, and vessel for the journey.

KEEL The bottom structure that runs the length of a ship in the very center, and to which the frames fasten.

LINER A large passenger ship that sails fixed routes ("lines").

LOOKOUTS The *Titanic* had six lookouts. Working in pairs they kept watch for other ships or obstacles ahead from the crow's nest on the foremast.

LOWER DECK This is the deck above the orlop deck. On the *Titanic* it was just above the waterline.

MAIDEN VOYAGE A ship's first journey.

MORSE CODE A telegraph code used to send messages. A system of dots and dashes represents letters and numbers.

A reconstruction of the first-class veranda café on the *Titanic*

ORLOP DECK The lowest deck.

PASSAGEWAY A walkway between cabins or other rooms.

POOP DECK A raised deck at the stern of a ship.

PORT The left-hand side of a ship.

PORTHOLE A small, usually round, window in the side of a ship. There were about 2,000 portholes and windows on the *Titanic*.

PROMENADE DECK An upper deck where people could take a walk.

PROPELLERS Three large propellers, driven by the engine, moved the *Titanic*.

A doll rescued from the *Titanic*

QUARTERMASTER A junior officer who was responsible for navigation.

READING ROOM A spacious, quiet room used for reading and writing.

RIVETS A short metal pin used to fasten things together.

ROYAL MAIL SHIP (RMS) A ship with a contract to carry mail from one place to another. The *Titanic* was carrying 3,364 sacks of mail.

RUDDER A vertical fin at the back of a ship, used for steering.

SALOON A large, public room on a ship. The first-class dining saloon was the largest room on the *Titanic*. It could seat 550 people.

SEA TRIALS Tests conducted at sea on a new ship to make sure the engines and steering are working well.

SHIPPING LINE A company that owns and runs passenger or freight ships.

SISTER SHIP One that is the same class and belongs to the same line.

SOS A Morse code distress call. The *Titanic* was one of the first ships to use this code.

STARBOARD The right-hand side of a ship.

STATEROOM A first-class private cabin.

STEAM TURBINE A machine that takes the energy of steam and turns it into the movement of a propeller.

STEERAGE The cheapest accommodation on a ship.

STERN The rear part of a ship.

STOKER A person who tends the furnaces on a steamship.

SUBMERSIBLE A submarine designed and equipped to carry out work deep on the seabed.

TRIMMER A person who wheels coal to the boilers to ensure that the remaining fuel is evenly distributed so the ship is balanced.

One of *Titanic*'s lifeboats

TURKISH BATH A steam bath.

WHEELHOUSE The enclosed structure on the bridge of a ship where officers steer the vessel.

WIRELESS OPERATORS The two people, employed by Marconi, who sent Morse code telegraph messages.

The *Titanic*'s bow on the seabed